NEGRO FOLK-SONGS

THE HAMPTON SERIES, BOOKS I–IV, COMPLETE

Natalie Curtis-Burlin

DOVER PUBLICATIONS, INC.
Mineola, New York

Bibliographical Note

This Dover edition, first published in 2001, is an unabridged but lightly restyled
compilation of the work originally published in four separate "books" by G. Schirmer,
Inc., New York, in 1918–19.
The original volumes have been repaginated to reflect their continuity in a composite edition, with new part titles added to identify each section. This edition also
adds a complete list of contents and a facsimile of the original group title page. Two
pages have been re-cut to improve text layout, and the author's note that reoccurred
in each "book" has been limited to its first appearance on p. vii. Original page refer-
ences in the footnotes have been corrected to correspond to the new layout.
We are grateful to the Indiana University Libraries, Bloomington, for providing a
rare copy of this work for republication.

International Standard Book Number: 0-486-41880-4

Manufactured in the United States of America
Dover Publications, Inc., 31 East 2nd Street, Mineola, N.Y. 11501

CONTENTS

Foreword to the Hampton Series   v

BOOK I: *Spirituals* 1

O ride on, Jesus
    Notes   3 / Music   7

Go down, Moses
    Notes   13 / Music   17

Couldn't hear nobody pray
    Notes   22 / Music   25

Good news, chariot's comin'!
    Notes   32 / Music   34

BOOK II: *Spirituals* 39

    Foreword   41

'Tis me, O Lord
    Notes   49 / Music   52

Listen to de Lambs
    Notes   57 / Music   61

O ev'ry time I feel de Spirit
    Notes   64 / Music   66

God's a-gwine ter move all de troubles away
    Notes   69 / Music   73

BOOK III: *Work- and Play-Songs* 83

    Foreword   85

    "Cotton in Song"   87

Cott'n-Pickin' Song
    Notes   89 / Music   93

Cott'n-Dance Song
    Notes   98 / Music   102

Cott'n-Packin' Song
    Notes   107 / Music   110

Corn-Shuckin' Song
    Notes   111 / Music   114

BOOK IV: *Work- and Play-Songs* 121

    Foreword and introductory notes   123

Peanut-Pickin' Song
    Notes   129 / Music   131

Hammerin' Song
    Notes   140 / Music   146

Lullaby
    Notes   149 / Music   150

"Chicka-Hanka"
    Notes   153 / Music   154

"Hyah, Rattler!"
    Notes   155 / Music   157

"Old Rags, Bottles, Rags!"
    Notes   156 / Music   157

'Liza-Jane
    Notes   158 / Music   160

FOREWORD

HAMPTON NORMAL AND AGRICULTURAL INSTITUTE, the pioneer industrial school for Negroes and Indians in America, was founded in 1868 by General Samuel Chapman Armstrong, who first conceived the idea that training in "labor for the sake of character" as well as for economic necessity, should be the initial step in the development of backward races. The school numbers about nine hundred students, drawn from all over the United States, while thousands of graduates have spread the Hampton spirit of service throughout the country and even far across the seas; for a few West Indians, Filipinos, Chinese, Japanese and Africans have also profited by Hampton's training and have gone back to their people to teach and lead them. Hampton believes in the good in every race; worthy traits are studied and developed; the folk-lore of Negroes and Indians is preserved and encouraged; and the singing of racial music is a part of the life of the school.

These notations of Negro folk-songs are faithful efforts to place on paper an exact record of the old traditional plantation songs *as sung by Negroes*. The harmonies are the Negroes' own. I have added nothing and I have striven to omit nothing. Every note in every voice was written down as sung by groups of Negroes, utterly untaught musically, who harmonized the old melodies as they sang, simply because it was natural for them to do so. The Negroes possess an intuitive gift for part-singing, which is an African inheritance. The music of most primitive or savage peoples usually consists in rhythm and melody only. But the native of Africa has a rudimentary harmonic sense, distinctly manifested in some of the African folk-songs that I have studied and recorded.[1] This instinct, transplanted to America and influenced by European music, has flowered into the truly extraordinary harmonic talent found in the singing of even the most ignorant Negroes of our Southern States. It seemed to me an obvious artistic duty to set down these intuitive harmonies and to note, in so far as possible, the emotional and dynamic qualities of Negro singing, as well as the forceful, yet subtle rhythmic peculiarities of the music.

No two groups of Negroes harmonize a song in the same way. These records are therefore musical photographs of particular groups, not composite pictures. The singing of plantation songs at Hampton is spontaneous and natural. No one teaches Negro songs. In one group of boys that sang for me, the tenor was learning to be a bricklayer and came to our meetings still grimed with toil; another was studying to teach school in a rural district; a third had learned the tinsmith's trade, and a fourth was ploughing the fields. These young men simply met and sang, each making up his own part and combining with the others till all together they produced a harmony that pleased them. In a general way, certain rudimentary harmonies for the old

[1] For a fuller exposition of the whole subject of Negro Song, see Foreword to Book II of this Series.

v

melodies have been more or less traditional at Hampton throughout the fifty years of the life of the school; yet the voice-progressions and even the versions of the melodies are strikingly individual with different singers. All around the grounds at Hampton the visitor comes across little groups of students singing together under the trees, or humming harmonies to one anothers' songs as they go to their work at the shops or in the fields. Music is literally "in the air." When I asked a newcomer from a remote district what part he sang in the "Spirituals" chanted by the whole school in Chapel on Sunday evenings, he answered naïvely: "O, sometimes I sings sopranner, an' sometimes I sings bay-uss; all depen's on de lay o' de song an' on how I feels." The enormous chorus of nine hundred Negro voices singing by nature, not by training; by ear and heart, and not by note; in perfect pitch, without accompaniment; each singer, no matter where he sits, taking any part he chooses in the harmonies of the whole—this chorus of folk-singers is among the most wonderful products of the United States!

Through leaving unspoiled this fresh, intuitive song-impulse in the Negro, and through cherishing the old music in its original purity and simplicity, Hampton has glorified the song of the slave as it has dignified the manual labor of the freedman, and is preserving in living form that spontaneous musical utterance which is the Negro's priceless contribution to the art of America.

Negro dialect is used in these notations, for to sing these typical Negro songs in words from which have been expunged the racial and picturesque quality seems as colorless, inartistic and unnatural as to sing Scotch or Irish ballads in anything but the vernacular, or German and French folk-songs in other than their own quaint and simple verse.

In trying to sing Negro dialect, white people should bear in mind that it is primarily a *legato* form of speech. The African languages of Bantu stock (from which great linguistic family came, probably, most of our American Negroes) are soft and musical in spite of the "clicks" in some of them; so that the transplanted Negro instinctively modified harsher sounds in English, sliding words together and leaving out whole syllables. "*Th*" being a difficult sound for most people not born to it, becomes "*D*" to the black man, but the *vowels* that follow should be pronounced as the white man pronounces them. For instance, "*the*," commonly spoken "*thuh*," is called by the Negro "*duh*" or "*d'*," not "*dee*." This should especially be borne in mind by white singers. For the sake of clarity I have adhered to the customary methods of dialect spelling except in a few cases where this seemed inadequate. To give to the verses the rhythm as sung, I have stressed the syllables accented by the music.

In singing four-part harmonies for male voices, the Hampton singers divide as follows: tenor (usually a very high voice); "lead" (or leader—who carries the melody); baritone, and bass. The Negroes say that in form their old songs usually consist in what they call "Chorus and Verses." The "Chorus," a melodic refrain sung by all, opens the song; then follows a verse sung as a solo, in free recitative; the chorus is repeated; then another verse; chorus again;—and so on until the chorus, sung for the last time, ends the song.

These songs, now traditional, were originally extemporaneous. They sprang into life as the expression of an emotion, of an experience, of a hope. The verses were made up as the occasion called for them—and a song was

vi

born.[1] As the songs passed from singer to singer and from one locality to another, they took on variants in words and melody; even to-day, two singers rarely sing a song in exactly the same way.

Like his African ancestors and in common with most simple people who live close to nature, the Negro sings at all times—at work, at play and at prayer. Into the "Spirituals," the prayer-songs of the days of slavery, was poured the aspiration of a race in bondage whose religion, primitive and intense, was their whole hope, sustenance and comfort, and the realm wherein the soul, at least, soared free. At stolen meetings in woods or in valleys, at secret gatherings on the plantations, the Negroes found outlet for their sorrows, their longings and their religious ecstasies. No one can hear these songs unmoved. The childlike simplicity of the verse in "Couldn't hear nobody pray"[2] and "Ev'ry time I feel de Spirit," but throws into sharper relief the touching, poignant poetry—a poetry born of hearts that sang beneath heavy burdens, and of a faith as radiant and certain as the sunrise. The Negro "Spirituals" rank with the great folk-music of the world, and are among the loveliest of chanted prayers.

Only after long familiarity with this music and innumerable hearings of the songs have I dared, with the additional aid of a phonograph, to set my notations on paper. This work of record—a reverent and dedicated love-labor—is pursued under the auspices of Hampton Institute. May it become part of Hampton's mission of friendship between the different races of the earth. For music is a common tongue which speaks directly to the heart of all mankind.

NOTE:—This collection of Negro Folk-Songs consists of four books, each containing four songs for male quartet. As the books will appear separately in serial publication, the descriptive notes accompanying each song are arranged in such a way as to make each volume independent of the other. Any slight repetition of facts with regard to Negro singing will, therefore, be understood.

NATALIE CURTIS-BURLIN.

---

[1] The origin of the best-known old songs has been lovingly traced by John Wesley Work, A. M., President of Fisk University, Nashville, Tennessee. His book, "Folk-Songs of the American Negro," is a fitting climax to the lifework of Fisk, which long ago sent out the "Jubilee Singers" with their offering of Negro songs. See also "Afro-American Folksongs," by H. E. Krehbiel (G. Schirmer : New York).

[2] See Book II, this Series

Nos. 6716, 6726, 6756, 6766

HAMPTON SERIES

NEGRO FOLK-SONGS

RECORDED BY

NATALIE CURTIS-BURLIN

Books I-II
Spirituals

Books III-IV
Work- and Play-Songs

Price, each, net, 50 cents
(In U. S. A.)

G. SCHIRMER, INC., NEW YORK

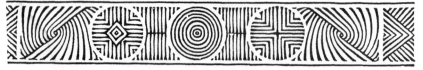

All royalties from the sale of these books go to Hampton Institute, Virginia, for the benefit of Negro education.

Reduced facsimile of the original title page.
G. Schirmer, Inc., New York, 1918–19

BOOK I

SPIRITUALS

O ride on, Jesus

Notes   3 / Music   7

Go down, Moses

Notes   13 / Music   17

Couldn't hear nobody pray

Notes   22 / Music   25

Good news, chariot's comin'!

Notes   32 / Music   34

O RIDE ON, JESUS

"O Ride on, Jesus,
Ride on, conquerin' King!"

The recording of this song is dedicated to the memory of
GENERAL SAMUEL CHAPMAN ARMSTRONG,
Founder of Hampton Institute

SHORTLY after the Civil War, when the South was flooded with the
pitiful and penniless freedmen, and when the increasing Westward
migration of white settlers had meant the clash of troops with the red
men and the bringing of Indian prisoners to Florida, it was General Armstrong
who took the first practical steps toward answering the question of what was
to be done with the two dark-skinned races, both of them ignorant and help-
less—ex-slaves, and Government "wards." With prophetic insight, Armstrong saw that Negroes and Indians must first of all be taught to stand on
their own feet, and to do this they must learn how to work, and how to support
themselves by work. To him the thing to be done was plain: so to train selected youth of the two races that they could become leaders of their people.

To-day, when manual and industrial training as a part of general education is no longer an experiment, it is difficult to realize that at the time General
Armstrong advocated it, the idea was without successful precedent in the
United States. Armstrong's principles, the inter-training of "hand, head and
heart," the teaching of "respect for labor," the correlation of study in the
classrooms with farming, home-making and trades—these were wholly new
theories of education, and they were greeted with skepticism and with wide
predictions of failure. That Armstrong succeeded in holding high the torch
of this illuminative idea in the early dark days of opposition was due not alone
to the intense conviction that burned in his own soul; that idea was bound
to triumph because of its truth and expediency and because it was based on
the sound principle of what Armstrong called "sanctified common-sense."
The real victory of Hampton is the fitting of men and women for life, mentally
and morally as well as industrially. And as the visitor to the school watches
the noontide daily drill of the students on the wide lawns that slope to the
water's edge, as he listens to the band played by boys, black and copper-
colored, and sees the stars and stripes flutter in the breeze upborne by loyal
black hands, he is moved with a sense of reverence for the heroic genius of
Armstrong; for these stalwart ranks of dark-skinned, self-respecting American manhood and womanhood that march past with ringing step and steady
eyes are those who have "come up out of deep darkness and wrong," the
children of slaves and so-called savages, transformed in a generation.

O RIDE ON, JESUS

Recorded from the singing of

Ira Godwin	("Lead")	Agriculture
Joseph Barnes	(Tenor)	Tinsmith
William Cooper	(Baritone)	Schoolteacher
Timothy Carper	(Bass)	Bricklayer

The version here recorded of this old song was brought to Hampton from St. Helena's Island, South Carolina, where an offshoot of the "Hampton Spirit" is practically demonstrated in the Penn Industrial School, situated in the heart of a black rural population and conducted by two devoted Hampton workers, Miss Rossa B. Cooley, principal, and Miss Grace Bigelow House, vice-principal. The Negroes on this Island are still primitive and their songs are very old. This one has a triumphant stride, and the climax of the verse "Ride on, conquerin' King!" when fairly shouted by a great Negro chorus, is as stirring as any "Hosanna in the highest." The whole song rings with the joy of certain salvation. The sinner on the "mourners' bench" has "come through": he has "bin baptize," and to-morrow he will be in "Galilee," whither he is already bound in spirit, shouting messages as he goes, to tell mother, father, sister, brother, preacher, deacon and all others, to meet him there. Each verse ends with the refrain that closes so many of the old songs— "Want t' go t' Hebb'n in de mo'nin'."

In "Old Plantation Hymns"[1] Rev. W. E. Barton says that "conspicuous among the religious songs of the colored people, as of the white people of the Cumberland Mountains, is the large group of 'Family Songs' in which the chief or only variation in the successive stanzas is the substitution of 'father,' 'mother,' or other relative in order." These songs, he tells us, are usually sung at the opening of religious services, and one can well see how, through their personal allusions, they would "warm" a "meet'n'." In the dignity of its melody this simple spiritual is a superb bit of music, while the last verse contains the sudden gleam of imagery that so often proclaims the ingenuous Negro folk-singer a true poet.

That many people in the North have had the opportunity to know the Negroes through their songs is due to the fact that, like Fisk University, which gave to the world the original Jubilee Singers, Hampton, too, sends her students during vacation far over the country to sing the old songs wherever meetings are held in behalf of the school; for regular campaigns to raise money for Negro education are organized and participated in by the faculty and the students of Hampton.[2] The recording of this song is taken from the singing of a self-organized quartet of Hampton boys, who had formed for Hampton meetings in the North during the summer of 1915. Each afternoon at odd hours taken from their work in shop, field or class, they came to

NOTE:—I printed the *verses* of this song with those of "God's a-gwine to move all de troubles away" (see Book II, this Series), in *Poetry*, December, 1917, accompanied by a little description.

[1] "Old Plantation Hymns." William E. Barton, D. D. Lamson Wolffe & Co., 1899.

[2] See "Negro Folk songs," Book II, this Series.

4

practice in a vacant room. The bricklayer was flecked with lime and mortar, the overalls of the tinsmith were covered with machine oil, but the boys flung themselves into their chairs and began to sing as unconcernedly as though they were simply resting from labor. They hummed over the song to be practiced, improvised their own harmonies, tried them out and fitted their parts together while I sat with pencil and paper astounded at the untaught facility and the unfaltering harmonic instinct of these natural singers, only one of whom had even a rudimentary knowledge of musical notation. They delighted in my task of trying to record their voices and they were always willing to repeat a phrase, often with much jolly laughter. It was curiously difficult, however, for tenor, baritone or bass to sing his part alone, because each was conscious of his own voice only as a bit of the whole. A *"part"* was not conceived as a separate thing, and whenever I tried to get one voice by itself, the "Lead," who carried the melody, was usually asked to make things easy by humming at the same time.

The making of phonographic records was a source of great amusement and interest to us all, and here too, in order to get one part separately recorded, the other three of the quartet would stand near the boy who was singing into the horn and hum their parts along with him. It is perhaps this inherent losing of self in a song that gives to primitive Negro part-singing such amazing unity—emotional, as well as musical.

For comparison, I have recorded a slightly different harmonic version as sung by the quartet known at Hampton as the "Big Quartet"— a group of four older men (Tynes, Crawley, Phillips and Wainwright), graduates of the school, who have been "singing for Hampton" for many years. I give the two versions as an interesting proof of the spontaneity of Negro song; for to the Negro, singing is a kind of melodious musing aloud, so that unconsciously it is a form of direct and individual expression. The Big Quartet was awarded a gold medal when the men sang at the Educational Department of the Panama-Pacific International Exposition in San Francisco. On hearing them, Percy Grainger exclaimed: "To think that, having toured all Europe, I should find the most perfect four-part singing of the world among these American Negroes!"

O RIDE ON,[1] JESUS

O Ride on, Jesus,
  Ride on, Jesus,
  Ride on, conquerin' King!
    I want t' go t' Hebb'n in de mo'n'in'.

Ef yo' see my Mother'
    O yes!
Jes' tell her fo' me,
    O yes!
For t' meet me t'-morrow in Galilee':
    Want t' go t' Hebb'n in de mo'n'in .

[1] The O on the word "on" is pronounced very long in Negro dialect, thus, "ōn" ("ohn").

5

O Ride on, Jesus,
  Ride on, Jesus,
  Ride on, conquerin' King!
   I want t' go t' Hebb'n in de mo'n'in'.

Ef you see <u>my</u> Father',[1]
   O yes!
Jes' tell <u>him</u> fo' <u>me</u>
   O yes!
For t' meet me t'-morrow in Galilee':
   Want t' go t' Hebb'n in de mo'n'in'.

O Ride on, Jesus,
  Ride on, Jesus,
  Ride on, conquerin' King!
   I want t' go t' Hebb'n in de mo'n'in'.

Ef yo' see <u>John</u> de Baptis'',
   O yes!
Jes' tell <u>him</u> fo' <u>me,</u>
   O yes!
Dat I's been to de ribber and I's been baptize'':
   Want t' go t' Hebb'n in de mo'n'in'.

O Ride on, Jesus,
  Ride on, Jesus,
  Ride on, conquerin' King!
   I want t' go t' Hebb'n in de mo'n'in'.

Ef yo' want t' go t' Hebb'n',
   O yes!
I'll-a tell yo' <u>how,</u>
   O yes!
Jes' keep yo' han's on de gospel <u>plow</u>:
   Want t' go t' Hebb'n in de mo'n'in'.

O Ride on, Jesus,
  Ride on, Jesus,
  Ride on, conquerin' King!
   I want t' go t' Hebb'n in de mo'n'in'.

[1] Other verses follow identical with these first two except for the substitution of the words "Sister" and "Brother" for "Mother" and "Father." This song may also be sung in broad dialect: "Ma Mudder," "Fader," "Brudder," etc.

O, ride on, Jesus!

Recorded and transcribed by Natalie Curtis-Burlin

* The *o* in the word "on" is pronounced very long in Negro dialect, *"ohn."*
** The melody is carried in the voice of the "Lead" (or "Leader"), printed in the piano-part in large type.
*** Very deep Negro voices take the low octave; this part may also be sung above with the baritone.

mo'n-in'! O, ride on, Je-sus, ride on, Je-sus, ride on,

mo'n-in'! O, ride on, Je-sus, ride on, Je-sus, ride on,

mo'n-in'! O, ride on, Je-sus, ride on, Je-sus, ride on,

mo'n-in'! O, ride on, Je-sus, ride on, Je-sus, ride on,

con-quer-in' King! I want t' go t' Heb-b'n in de mo'n-in'!

con-quer-in' King! I want t' go t' Heb-b'n in de mo'n-in'!

con-quer-in' King! I want t' go t' Heb-b'n in de mo'n-in'!

con-quer-in' King! I want t' go t' Heb-b'n in de mo'n-in'!

Rather spirited, calling
jubilantly

SOLO

O yes!   O yes!   O yes!   O yes!

1. Ef yo'   see my Moth-er,   O yes! Jes' tell her fo' me
2. Ef yo'   see my Fa-ther,   Jes' tell him fo' me
3. Ef yo'   see my Sis-ter,   Jes' tell her fo' me
4. Ef yo'   see my Broth-er,   Jes' tell him fo' me

O yes! for t'

O yes!   O yes!

O yes!   O yes!

mf very legato

Chorus *D.C.*

Want t' go t' Heb-b'n in de mo'n-in.'

Verse 5
SOLO

meet me t'-morrow in Gal-i-lee: Want t' go t' Heb-b'n in de mo'n-in.' O, Ef yo'

Want t' go t' Heb-b'n in de mo'n-in.'

Want t' go t' Heb-b'n in de mo'n-in.'

* May also be sung in broad dialect: "Mud-der, Fader, Brudder."

** May also be harmonized thus:

*** If sung by chorus, instead of quartet, the solo voice does *not* sing: "O yes!"

**** May also be harmonized thus:

9

see John de Bap-tis',' O yes! Jes' tell him fo' me O yes! Dat I's

been to de rib-ber an I's been bap-tize':– Want t' go t' Heb b'n in de mo'n-in.' O,

Verse 6

Ef yo' want t' go t' Heb-b'n, O yes! I'll-a tell' yo' how; O yes! Jes'

keep yo' han's on de gos-pel plow. Want t' go t' Heb-b'n in de mo'n-in.' O,

Sometimes, after the last chorus, at the very end of the song, the final notes may be suddenly harmonized thus:

Want t' go t' Heb-b'n in de mo'n - in.'

Want t' go t' Heb-b'n in de mo'n - in.'

Want t' go t' Heb-b'n in de mo'n - in.'

Want t' go t' Heb-b'n in de mo'n - in.'

The refrain is sung as follows by the Hampton "Big Quartet" (Messrs. Tynes, Crawley, Avery and Wainwright):

The verses are sung as follows by Tynes, who usually sings Tenor instead of "lead," but whose fluent melodic talent makes his versions worthy of record.

Verses 1-4.

SOLO
Ef yo' see my Moth-er, O yes! Jes'

CHORUS   SOLO
tell her fo' me O yes! For to meet me to-mor-row in

CHORUS   CHORUS D.C.
Gal-i-lee:— Want t' go t' Heb-b'n in de mo'n-in.' O,

Verse 5
SOLO
Ef yo' see John Bap-tis,' O yes! Jes'

CHORUS   SOLO
tell him fo' me O yes! Dat I's been to de rib-ber an'

CHORUS   CHORUS D.C.
been bap-tize':— Want t' go t' Heb-b'n in de mo'n-in'. O,

Verse 6
SOLO
Ef yo' want t' go t' Heb-b'n, O yes! I'll-a

CHORUS   SOLO
tell yo' how, O yes! 'Jes' keep yo' han's on de

CHORUS   CHORUS D.C.
gos-pel plow:— Want t' go t' Heb-b'n in de mo'n-in'.

12

GO DOWN, MOSES

"Go down, Moses,
Tell old Pharaoh
Let my people go!"

The recording of this song is dedicated to the memory of

BOOKER T. WASHINGTON

FOUNDER OF TUSKEGEE INSTITUTE, ALABAMA, WHERE COLORED STUDENTS
ARE TAUGHT BY THE MORE ADVANCED OF THEIR OWN RACE AND WHERE LOVE
OF THE LAND AND PRIDE IN ITS DEVELOPMENT LINK THE NEGRO WITH THE
PROGRESS OF THE SOUTH.

MANY years ago a colored lad, ragged and worn, arrived at Hampton, having struggled thither on foot five hundred miles, sleeping in the open, begging rides from passing wagons and earning his food by labor on the way. He had no money nor could he meet all the qualifications for admission to the institute, but so earnest was his plea for an education and so convincing his eagerness to work, that the teacher, leaving the room, bade the waiting boy dust and put it in order. Immaculate cleanliness awaited the master when he returned. Into the simple task the boy had thrown his whole determination. His character had been tested, and Booker Washington was admitted.

His life became an embodiment of Armstrong's ringing motto: "Dare to do the impossible!" Who, indeed, could have foreseen that a dilapidated little church, which some thirty years ago barely housed thirty Negro students, could become through the consecrated effort and executive ability of one colored man the great Tuskegee Institute, comprising to-day over a hundred fine buildings covering many acres of ground, where a thousand and more pupils are annually taught.

Among the trustees of Tuskegee are some of the most important white men in the United States. Throughout the world Booker Washington became known as one of the greatest exponents of industrial education; high tributes here and abroad were awarded him and honorary degrees were conferred upon him by Harvard and Dartmouth colleges.

The sixteen thousand colored men and women who have been directly benefited by Tuskegee, and also the many members of the National Negro Business League founded by Washington—these bear vital testimony to the practical, constructive and adaptive genius of the author of "Up from Slavery."

Teacher in the highest sense, orator and patriot, Booker Washington was a prophet among his own people and one of the great leaders of mankind.

GO DOWN, MOSES

First Version

Recorded from the singing of

Ira Godwin	("Lead")	Agriculture
Joseph Barnes	(Tenor)	Tinsmith
William Cooper	(Baritone)	Schoolteacher
Timothy Carper	(Bass)	Bricklayer

Second Version

From the singing of the "Big Quartet"
Messrs. Tynes, Crawley, Avery and Wainwright

THIS song is full of that quality of elemental drama that underlies primitive music born of profound emotion. It is one of the best known of the Spirituals and deserves to rank with the great songs of the world. The melody may be very old[1]: it sounds as though it might have sprung from the heart of ancient Africa; and so indelibly does it carve its outline on the memory that it could well outlive generations of men and be carried from land to land. Like that Negroid influence that had its part in the shaping of the culture of the Egyptians, the Semites and the earliest Greeks, this melody will live on, moving from race to race—one of the immortals in art.

The American-Negro verses, "Go Down, Moses," were born, of course, of slavery in this country. In the sorrows of Israel in Egypt, oppressed and in bondage, the Negro drew a natural poetic analogy to his own fate, and this song is not the only one that refers to the story of Moses.[2] Rarely does the slave dare to sing openly of slavery or of the hope for any other freedom than that promised by the release of death: through the allegory of the Bible, he tells of his firm faith for a like deliverance from the hand of the white Pharaoh.

The chorus at Hampton sings this spiritual with an immense body of sustained tone. All in unison, without accompaniment of any kind, nine hundred voices chant the command "Go Down, Moses," like a single voice, overwhelming in dignity and power. Perhaps because of the great weight of sound, the chorus has formed the tradition of dwelling on the last note in each of the first two bars with an almost awesome solemnity. At the end of the phrase, the sudden bursting into a triumphant major chord stirs the imagination. It comes like a rift of light, like a vision of the splendor and

[1] Though its origin is as yet untraced, John Wesley Work of Fisk University says that Hebrews have recognized in this Negro song a resemblance to an old Jewish Chant, "Cain and Abel," while Negroes, on their side, have identified the Hebrew song with their own "Go Down, Moses." This may be but a musical coincidence, or more probably, one of the many instances of how different peoples, influenced by analogous conditions (climatic or cultural), react artistically in similar ways to the stimulus of nature. Or, on the other hand, the incident described by Mr. Work may add emphasis to the statement in the Foreword to Book II of this series concerning the relation between Negro and Semitic cultures on the Dark Continent.

[2] See refrain: "I never intend to die in Egypt Land"; also the songs "Hammering Judgment" and "Bye and Bye" (Calhoun Plantation Songs: Emily Halowell) and "Turn back Pharaoh's Army," Fisk Collection, Jubilee Singers, etc., etc.

See also "Antebellum Sermon." Collected poems by Paul Lawrence Dunbar (Dodd, Mead & Co., N. Y.).

authority of Jehovah, and it heightens the emphasis of the final words, "Let my people go!" This chord effect is not used everywhere, and I have yet to ascertain whether it is peculiar to Hampton or if it may also be heard in other parts of the South. The free declamation of the verses is, of course, variously rendered. Among Southern Negroes—true folk-singers—*I have never heard it in anything but syncopated form.*

The "Big Quartet" gives the opening bars in strict time, as I have indicated in the second recording, and this is, of course, the more common rendering everywhere. But some of the Hampton Quartets, taking their inspiration from the great chorus, sing the refrain with the same long-drawn, almost ritualistic cadences, and I have written this version in detail because in its dramatic breadth it exemplifies the unconscious way in which musical phrases grow and expand among folk-singers. As the song is well known, the comparison of different versions, indigenously Negro, can but enrich the study of Negro primitive art.

GO DOWN, MOSES[1]

Go down, Moses',
> *'Way down Egyp''¹ Lan',*
Tell ol' Pharaoh'¹
> *Le' ma people' go!*

When Isr'el was in Egyp' Lan'
> *Le' ma people' go!*
Oppress' so hard dey could not stan
> *Le' ma people' go!*

Go down, Moses',
> *'Way down Egyp'' Lan',*
Tell ol' Pharaoh'
> *Le' ma people' go!*

When dey had reached de odder shore
> *Le' ma people' go!*
Dey sang a song of triumph o'er
> *Le' ma people' go!*

Go down, Moses',
> *'Way down Egyp'' Lan',*
Tell ol' Pharaoh'
> *Le' ma people' go.*

[1] Pronounced "Mosis," "Ejup," and sometimes "Pharioh."

A fuller version of the words of this song is given in an older Hampton collection by Thomas P. Fenner, as follows:[1]

> When Israel was in Egypt's land,
>> Let my people go;
> Oppressed so hard they could not stand,
>> Let my people go.

Chorus
> Go down, Moses,
>> 'Way down in Egypt's land;
> Tell ole Pharaoh,
>> Let my people go.

> Thus saith the Lord, bold Moses said,
>> Let my people go;
> If not I'll smite your first-born dead,
>> Let my people go.
>>> (*Chorus*)

> No more shall they in bondage toil,
>> Let my people go;
> Let them come out with Egypt's spoil,
>> Let my people go.
>>> (*Chorus*)

> The Lord told Moses what to do,
>> Let my people go;
> To lead the children of Israel thro',
>> Let my people go.
>>> (*Chorus*)

> When they had reached the other shore,
>> Let my people go;
> They sang a song of triumph o'er,
>> Let my people go.
>>> (*Chorus*)

[1] See "Religious Folk-songs of the Negro" (The Hampton Institute Press, Hampton, Virginia).

A book of "Jubilee and Plantation Songs" published by Oliver Ditson in 1887, and "Jubilee Songs" published by Biglow & Main, N. Y., offer as many as twenty-five verses, while some versions contain upwards of thirty.

Go Down, Moses

* The voice of the "Lead" (or Leader) carries the melody of the song and is printed in the piano part in large type.
** Notes marked with fermate ⌢ are almost equal to half-notes (𝅗𝅥 = 𝅘𝅥) Yet this traditional manner of declaiming these opening phrases is not universal. Many of the Hampton singers give out the words "Go down, Moses" more nearly in strict time. However, the half-notes on the words "'Way down" are always drawn out.
*** Pronounced "Mosis". **** Pronounced "Ejup".
***** Often pronounced "Parioh", and sometimes sung with a little melodic from: Phar-ioh

* Long pause, longer than first time, giving an emphatic finality to this closing refrain of the Chorus. Each time the Chorus is sung, it ends in this impressive manner.

* When this song is sung by full Chorus, the solo voice takes the melody with the "Lead" in the refrain "Le' ma people go!" In the male quartet, the solo voice, being bass, takes the bass part in the refrain, the melody being carried in the two inner voices.

20

The Hampton"Big Quartet", consisting of Messrs. Tynes, Crawley, Avery and Wainwright, sings the opening phrases "Go down, Moses", <u>without</u> the pauses on the last notes of the bars. The command is sung loud, and the Ab chord is sung *decrescendo*. The solo voice in this Quartet declaims the narrative verses as follows, without dialect.

21

COULDN'T HEAR NOBODY PRAY

"Hallelulah, troubles over,
Crossing over into Canaan."

The recording of this song is dedicated to the memory of
HOLLIS BURKE FRISSELL*, Principal of Hampton Institute

UNDER WHOSE PATIENT, WISE AND DEVOTED GUIDANCE THE "HAMPTON IDEA"
HAS COME TO FULL FRUITION AND HAS TAKEN DEEP ROOT IN MANY SCHOOLS FOR
WHITES AS WELL AS BLACKS, ALL OVER THIS CONTINENT. SCATTERING ITS
SEEDS TO DISTANT LANDS, IT IS NOW AN INFLUENCE IN THE TRAINING-SCHOOLS
OF CHINA, INDIA, AFRICA AND WHEREVER THE PROBLEMS OF INTER-RACIAL
ADJUSTMENT PRESS FOR FAR-SEEING AND JUST SOLUTION. IN THE DEVELOP-
MENT OF HAMPTON BEYOND EVEN ITS FOUNDERS' DREAM; IN THE STEADY AND
SOUND ADVANCE OF THE NEGRO AND INDIAN RACES IN AGRICULTURE AND SELF-
SUPPORT; IN THE GROWTH OF UNDERSTANDING AND FRIENDLY FEELING BE-
TWEEN WHITES AND NEGROES AND INDIANS AND WHITES, WE TRACE THE
GENTLE THOUGH FORCEFUL SPIRIT OF ARMSTRONG'S GREAT SUCCESSOR, WHO
HAS WELL BEEN CALLED "DOCTOR OF HUMAN KINDNESS."

*Since the writing of the above, the United States has lost one of its greatest educators
and the Negro and Indian races their ablest white leader in the death of Dr. Frissell on
August 5, 1917.

COULDN'T HEAR NOBODY PRAY

Recorded from the singing of the "Big Quartet"

Freeman W. Crawley	("Lead")
Charles H. Tynes	(Tenor)
William A. Avery	(Baritone)
John A. Wainwright	(Bass)

The lyric beauty of this music is equalled by the poetic suggestion of
the words, which bring before the hearer the emotions of the lonely soul, afar
in the valley with "his burden and his Saviour"—praying, and being at last
received into the promised land.

Sometimes such a song as this reflects a genuine experience, a real prayer
in the valley; sometimes an inner event is expressed in allegory. Indeed,
the "valley," in many a Negro song, is the symbolic place of prayer and of
sadness and struggle, as the mountain-top is that of exaltation. These are
wholly natural symbols that might be seized upon by any member of the
human family, regardless of race. Yet some of the spirituals reveal that
"John de Bunyan"[1] was not unknown to black singers, and we can well imagine
how the figurative outline of Pilgrim's Progress would impress the eager
mind of some listening slave.

This spiritual is, however, sheer poetry, and should find a place in the
literature as well as in the music of our land.

[1] See "Calhoun Plantation Songs," Emily Hallowell.

22

An' *I couldn't hear nobod'y pray.*
                              O Lord!

Couldn't hear nobod'y pray,
   O *—way down yonder*
     By myself,
I couldn't hear nobod'y pray,

In the valley,
    Couldn't hear nobod'y pray,
On my knees,
    Couldn't hear nobod'y pray,
With my burden,*
    Couldn't hear nobod'y pray,
An' my Saviour,
    Couldn't hear nobod'y pray.

     O Lord!

I couldn't hear nobod'y pray,
       O Lord!

Couldn't hear nobod'y pray.
   O—way down yonder
     By myself,
I couldn't hear nobod'y pray.

Chilly waters,
    Couldn't hear nobod'y pray,
In the Jerdan,†
    Couldn't hear nobod'y pray,
Crossing over,
    Couldn't hear nobod'y pray,
Into Canaan,
    Couldn't hear nobod'y pray.

     O Lord!

I couldn't hear nobod'y pray,
       O Lord!

Couldn't hear nobod'y pray.
   O—way down yonder
     By myself,
I couldn't hear nobod'y pray.

*Another version gives the text of this first verse thus:
    In the valley
    On my knees,
    With my burden
    So lonesome!

†*Jordan*, pronounced by the Negroes "*Jerdan*."

Hallejuh!
    Couldn't hear nobod'y pray,
Troubles over,
    Couldn't hear nobod'y pray,
In the Kingdom,
    Couldn't hear nobod'y pray,
With my Jesus,
    Couldn't hear nobod'y pray.

   O Lord!

I couldn't hear nobod'y pray,
        O Lord!

Couldn't hear nobod'y pray.
 O—way down yonder
  By myself,
I couldn't hear nobod'y pray.

Couldn't hear nobody pray

* The melody is carried in the voice of the "Lead" (or Leader) printed in the piano-part in large type.
** The bass in this phrase, whenever repeated, comes well to the fore.

* Throughout the song, whenever this bar is sung, there is a slight pause on this note. The paus
is not long enough to be actually felt as such, but it is distinctly apparent with the metronome

27

* The o in the word "on" is pronounced very long in Negro dialect,"ohn".

** Jordan River is usually called "Jerdan" by Negroes of the Southern States.

28

29

* At the end, after all three verses have been sung with the Choral ending, the chorus is again sung through pianissimo from this bar on, finishing on a long note, which dies away.

At the end, the chorus is again sung through, pianissimo from the ✳, previous page.

GOOD NEWS, CHARIOT'S COMIN'!

"Good news, Chariot's comin'!
An' I don't want her leave-a me behin'."

This song-record is dedicated to

ROBERT RUSSA MOTON

AN AMERICAN NEGRO OF DIRECT AFRICAN DESCENT, GRADUATE OF HAMPTON, LIFELONG FRIEND OF BOOKER WASHINGTON AND PRESENT PRINCIPAL OF TUSKEGEE INSTITUTE. AS FORMER COMMANDANT AT HAMPTON, AS SECRETARY OF THE NEGRO RURAL SCHOOL FUND BOARD OF THE JEANES FOUNDATION, AS TRUSTEE OF SEVERAL NEGRO INSTITUTIONS AND AS PRESIDENT OF THE NEGRO ORGANIZATION SOCIETY (WHICH TOUCHES THE LIVES OF OVER 350,000 BLACKS IN VIRGINIA ALONE), ROBERT MOTON HAS LONG BEEN A POWER IN THE ADVANCE OF HIS PEOPLE. FEW MEN GRASP WITH SUCH CALM, SOUND JUDGMENT THE PROBLEMS RELATING TO MASSES OF NEGROES LIVING AND STRUGGLING SIDE BY SIDE WITH THE DOMINANT WHITE RACE. HE HAS CONSTANTLY URGED COLORED MEN TO CULTIVATE RACE PRIDE; TO UNITE IN ALL QUESTIONS OF RACE-UPLIFT; TO LEAD WHOLESOME AND MORAL LIVES; TO SEEK DEVELOPMENT THROUGH HONEST WORK OF ALL KINDS; TO BUILD FOR THEMSELVES BETTER HOMES AND SCHOOLS, AND ABOVE ALL TO STRIVE ONWARD IN WILLING COÖPERATION WITH THEIR WHITE FRIENDS. HIS POISE, HIS SIMPLICITY, FRANKNESS AND BREADTH OF VIEW HAVE WON HIM THE CONFIDENCE OF BOTH RACES.

No visitor to Hampton in past years can forget the tall, inspiring man who sang in the great chorus with uplifted hand, nor the power and sweetness of the voice of the "Lead"—Robert Moton.

GOOD NEWS, CHARIOT'S COMIN'!

Recorded from the singing of the "Big Quartet"

Freeman W. Crawley	("Lead")
Charles H. Tynes	(Tenor)
Samuel E. Phillips	(Baritone)
John A. Wainwright	(Bass)

This song, with its glad heralding and repetition of "Good News!" is sung with quick enthusiasm and exuberant spontaneity, and with an echoing sound of acclamation. It is one of those Negro songs in which childlike joy reaches religious ecstasy, when eager voices, full of promise, describe the "starry crown," "long white robe" and "silver slippers" in that heaven which was the dream of the slave. The musical picture of the chariot drawing near in swift descent while hailed and welcomed, is vivid and dramatic in its directness; yet it has that rudimentary simplicity of thought, feeling and expression which is at once the charm and the virtue of the true folk-song.

Like the basso of the Russian choir, the Negro bass is singularly powerful and wide-ranged. Sometimes the voice plunges into almost incredible depths, so that the vibrations seem to move in long waves like the low notes of an organ. Yet always the higher tones are unforced, full and sweet-timbred. In this song the bass part is prominent; full of dynamic emphasis, it solidly sustains the freshness and vigor of the upper voices.

Good news, Char'iot's comin'!
Good news, Char'iot's comin'!
Good news, Char'iot's comin'!
An' I don't want her leave-a me behin'.

Dar's a long white robe in de Hebb'n, I know.
Dar's a long white robe in de Hebb'n, I know,
Dar's a long white robe in de Hebb'n, I know,
An' I don't want her leave-a me behin'.

Dar's a starry crown in de Hebb'n, I know.
Dar's a starry crown in de Hebb'n, I know,
Dar's a starry crown in de Hebb'n, I know,
An' I don't want her leave-a me behin'.

Good news, Char'iot's comin'!
Good news, Char'iot's comin'!
Good news, Char'iot's comin'!
An' I don't want her leave-a me behin'.

Dar's a golden harp in de Hebb'n, I know.
Dar's a golden harp in de Hebb'n, I know,
Dar's a golden harp in de Hebb'n, I know,
An' I don't want her leave-a me behin'.

Dar's silver slippers in de Hebb'n, I know.
Dar's silver slippers in de Hebb'n, I know,
Dar's silver slippers in de Hebb'n, I know,
An' I don't want her leave-a me behin'

Good news, Char'iot's comin'!
Good news, Char'iot's comin'!
Good news, Char'iot's comin'!
An' I don't want her leave-a me behin'.

Good News, Chariot's Comin'!

Chorus
Freshly, with vigor, spirit and enthusiasm

Tenor

Lead *

Baritone

Bass

Freshly, with vigor, spirit and enthusiasm (♩=96)

Piano
(only for
rehearsal)

* The voice of the "Lead"(or Leader) carries the melody of the song and is printed in the piano-part in large type.

37

star-ry crown in de Heb-ben, I know, Dar's a star-ry crown in de
sil-ver slip-pers in de Heb-ben, I know, Dar's sil-ver slip-pers in de

star-ry crown in de Heb-ben, I know, Dar's a star-ry crown in de
sil-ver slip-pers in de Heb-ben, I know, Dar's sil-ver slip-pers in de

star-ry crown in de Heb-ben, I know, Dar's a star-ry crown in de
sil-ver slip-pers in de Heb-ben, I know, Dar's sil-ver slip-pers in de

1st Chorus *D.C.*

Heb-ben, I know, An' I don't want her leave-a me be-hin'.
Heb-ben, I know, An' I don't want her leave-a me be-hin'.

Heb-ben, I know, An' I don't want her leave-a me be-hin'.
Heb-ben, I know, An' I don't want her leave-a me be-hin'.

An' I don't want her leave-a me be-hin'.
An' I don't want her leave-a me be-hin'.

Heb-ben, I know, An' I don't want her leave-a me be-hin'.
Heb-ben, I know, An' I don't want her leave-a me be-hin'.

38

BOOK II

SPIRITUALS

"These four songs are arranged in this sequence
for practical use on concert programs, and have been selected
because of their contrasting character, sentiment and tonality."

Foreword   41

'Tis me, O Lord

Notes   49 / Music   52

Listen to de Lambs

Notes   57 / Music   61

O ev'ry time I feel de Spirit

Notes   64 / Music   66

God's a-gwine ter move
all de troubles away

Notes   69 / Music   73

FOREWORD

It has been the object of the author to make this little foreword as non-technical as possible, couching it in language that may easily be comprehended by the layman.

IN music there can be scarcely a task more reverent than that of scribe to the unlettered song of a people. A folk-song, expressing as it does the soul of a race, is in that sense a holy thing, for through it sings the voice of humanity—humanity, as much greater than the individual as the universe is greater than a star. To touch the People's song and not artificialize, change or cheapen it in the written expression—here is a work that calls for humility, for selfless dedication, and for warm human sympathy as well as artistic training. One must love the People as well as their music, and one must feel *with them* in order first to understand and then to write what has risen from the depths of racial experience. For the folk-song, of all music, is insistent in its demand for truth.

Truth!—Truth in art as in life, the revulsion against artificiality and the longing for simplicity, the emphasis on the thing said rather than on elaborations in the manner of saying it;—may we not hope that this will be one of the by-products of the war which has drawn together men of different races and creeds in the sharing of common, elemental emotions? For the ever-widening interest in folk-music *as such*, and the need for popular singing, are prophetic.

This work of collecting and recording Negro folk-songs was begun some years ago at the request of a group of earnest colored men, one of whom was Robert R. Moton, now principal of Tuskegee, who asked me to do for the music of their race what I had tried to do for that of the Indian: to present it with entire genuineness and in a form of publication that could readily be grasped by all people. I therefore set myself the same uncompromising ideal that I had striven to follow in all my previous notations of unrecorded folk-music—I endeavored to put in written form, without addition or change of any kind, the true folk-song, spirit and sound, just as it springs from the hearts and the lips of the folk-singers. In other words, I tried to reflect on paper completely, but only, *what the people sang.* As most of the Negro songs are in essence group-songs, and as Negro group-singing, which is spontaneous and almost inevitable where two or three colored people are gathered together, is usually part-singing, I determined to record every part as sung, and also to seize, as nearly as notation would permit, each nuance, rhythmic and dynamic.

To this end the little Edison phonograph that had accompanied me to many an Indian reservation, was now set up in Virginia. I lack entire faith in the study of wax records afar from the live voice of the singer; perfect cylinders can be made only under perfect mechanical and acoustical conditions, carefully prepared. Besides, it has always seemed to me of the highest importance that the transcriber of folk-music should live for the time being in the midst of the folk-singers, where he can drink in the atmosphere and spirit of the instinctive song of un-selfconscious people—a type of music which is by its very nature furthermost removed from all idea of mechanism. Thus the folk-

41

song (no longer a musical specimen like a butterfly on a pin) becomes a part of the recorder's own being, so that he thinks and feels musically in the same rhythms and accents with the singers, till at last there grows up within him an almost intuitive conception of an adequate written form.   Then it is that the phonograph with its wealth of recorded detail takes its true place as an invaluable adjunct to the higher spiritual task of assimilating the folk-idiom and translating it mentally into terms of notation.

Though I had previously travelled widely in the South, I now made pro-tracted stays each year and heard the most primitive Negroes sing in crude log churches, in open-air "meet'n's" and in the fields; yet before I attempted to notate this music, I wanted to reach back if possible to the very well-springs of Negro song, and so I devoted a year to the study of native African music which I carefully recorded from the singing of two Africans: Madikane Cele, a Zulu from Natal, and Kamba Simango, from the Ndau tribe of Portuguese East Africa.   Both these young men had come directly from the Dark Continent to the United States to seek industrial training at Hampton Institute in order that they might carry back to their people the sorely needed knowledge of trades and developed agriculture.   It was my original intention to include the African songs in this Negro collection, so that students might trace the links between the music of black Africa and that evolved by the Negro in our Southern States.   But I found the native songs—like those of the North American Indian—so interwoven with the religion and customs, the legends, and indeed the whole life of the people, as to be hardly comprehensible with-out a description of the ceremony of which they are a part, or of the racial idea that called them into life.   So as I studied a book grew under my hands, demanding separate publication as "African Songs from the Dark Continent."[1]

Strangely enough, I had begun this research before the appearance of Mr. H. E. Krehbiel's valuable volume: "Afro-American Folksongs"[2]; so that the few conclusions independently reached by me as to the relation of Negro music to the parent stem, now form, in a sense, an unconscious con-firmatory sequel.

That Negro folk-song is indeed an offshoot from an African root, nobody who has heard Africans sing or even beat the drum can deny.   The American Negroes are sprung, of course, from many tribes; but whereas the native traffic in slaves and captives brought individuals from widely separated parts of the continent to the coasts and thus to the European slavers, the great mass of Negroes that filled the slave ships destined for America probably belonged —according to some authorities—to the big linguistic stock called Bantu, comprising some fifty million people south of the equator.   The Zulu and Ndau tribes, whose songs I studied, are of this stock.   Yet, as there are over a hundred million Negroes on the Dark Continent, whose different traits are probably represented in some form in this country, all statements as to musical derivations could be made with final authority only by one who had studied comprehensively the music of many different tribes *in Africa*.   This much, however, one may most emphatically affirm: though the Negro, trans-planted to other lands, absorbed much musically from a surrounding civiliza-

[1]In press with Doubleday, Page & Co., New York.

[2]*Afro-American Folksongs*, H E. Krehbiel.   Published by G. Schirmer, N. Y.

42

tion, yet the characteristics which give to his music an interest worthy of particular study are precisely those which differentiate Negro songs from the songs of the neighboring white man; they are racial traits, and the black man brought them from the Dark Continent.

The most obvious point of demarcation between Negro music and European is found, of course, in the rhythm. The simpler rhythms natural to the white man (I speak of folk-music, the people's song, not of the elaborate creations of trained musicians) are usually even and symmetrical. Throughout Western Europe and in English and Latin countries, the accents fall as a rule on the stressed syllables of the spoken tongue and on the regular beats of the music. The opposite is the case in Negro songs: here the rhythms are uneven, jagged, and, at a first hearing, eccentric, for the accents fall most frequently on the short notes and on the naturally *unstressed* beats, producing what we call "syncopation"[1] of a very intricate and highly developed order. The peculiarity of this syncopation is best explained to the layman by drawing attention to the way in which the natural rhythms of the English language are distorted to fit the rhythm of Negro music: where the white man would sing, "*Go* down, *Mo*ses," the Negro chants, "Go *down*, M*o*ses," while a phrase like "See my Mother" becomes in the mouth of the colored singer "See *my* M*other*." These identical accents are found in even the wordless vowel refrains of native African songs. Rhythmically the Negro folk-song has far more variety of accent than the European; it captivates the ear and the imagination with its exciting vitality and with its sense of alertness and movement. For this reason Negro rhythms and white man imitations of them popularized as "rag-time" have spread far and wide and have conquered the world to-day. The black man has by nature a highly organized rhythmic sense. A totally uneducated Negro, dancing or playing the bones, is often a consummate artist in rhythm, performing with utter abandon and yet with flawless accuracy. My African informant, Kamba Simango, thought nothing of singing one rhythm, beating another with his hands and dancing a third—and all at once!

Melodically as well as rhythmically, American Negro songs possess distinct characteristics. One of these is a very prevalent use of the pentatonic or five-tone scale, corresponding to the black keys of the piano.[2] In my recordings of Negro songs the melodies of six out of the eight Spirituals published in this collection are in the pentatonic scale, as are all three of the Cotton-Songs. Whereas, of the "Work- and Play-Songs,"[3] the Peanut-Picking Song, The Corn-Shucking Song, the Lullaby, the Hammering-Song and the Dance-Song ("Stealin'-Partners") are also all five-tone. Though I am publishing only songs typically Negro, discarding those that seem more obviously white-man-influenced, yet I was myself surprised to find the pentatonic scale so prominent. If one comes upon a group of colored men unconsciously humming or whistling at work, most often it is the five-tone scale that utters their musical thoughts. This scale—along with other scales—is heard in

[1]The Century Dictionary gives the following definition of syncopation: "Act, process or result of inverting the rhythmic accent by beginning a tone or tones on an unaccented beat or pulse and sustaining them into an accented one so that the proper emphasis on the latter is more or less transferred back or anticipated. Syncopation may occur wholly within a measure, or may extend from measure to measure."

[2]See H. E. Krehbiel's analysis of the scales used in American Negro Songs, Chapters VI and VII, "*Afro-American Folksongs*" (G. Schirmer. N. Y.).

[3]See Books III and IV of this series.

43

black Africa also, and in the music of many simple peoples in different parts of the world. Indeed, just as totally unrelated races at certain stages of culture seem to trace many of the same rudimentary symbols and designs on pottery and in textiles, so in music, the archaic simplicity of the five-tone scale would seem almost a basic human art-instinct. Yet the highly developed civilization and the carefully defined musical systems of China and other nations of the farthest East retain the pentatonic scale in wide use, the Chinese, in their philosophical and mystical theories of music, linking the five tones symbolically with the heavenly bodies. It is surprising how much variety can be achieved with these five tones. One of the most graceful melodies that I know in all music is the popular Chinese "Lily Song" which I recorded from a Chinese actor and which possesses the sheer beauty of outline and the firm delicacy of a Chinese drawing. Indeed, the melodic possibilities of the five-tone scale, containing a charm absolutely peculiar to that scale, instead of being limited, seem almost endless.

American Negro music is, however, by no means restricted to this tonality, for we find a broad indulgence in the major and minor modes of modern art, and also there are many songs in which occur tones foreign to those scales, most common of which is perhaps the minor, or flat, seventh. In the song "Listen to de Lambs" in this collection, the opening phrase is typically pentatonic in character (the semitones in the second phrase are undoubtedly modern); then later, the voice of the "Lead" or leader rises on the words "want t' go t' Hebb'n when I die" to the flat seventh so often heard in the old slave-songs —an interval which conveys a singular richness of beauty to the melody. Then, too, there are songs framed in the scale with a sharp fourth; and we also find, though more rarely in Negro music, the augmented interval of three semitones. Those of us who have noted Arabic folk-songs are accustomed to associate this latter interval with Semitic music; occurring as it does in African music also, it reminds us of the contact between the black population of Africa and the Semitic peoples in the white North of the continent whose caravan trade brought them into communication with the more savage interior, while their ships touched at ports along the coasts and even landed colonists on the Eastern shores, where Arab trade across the Red Sea must have existed since early Bible times. As the age-old slave traffic brought captives from African tribes out from the heart of black Africa to the North, we can readily see how, since the very dawn of history, Negro and Semitic cultures must have touched. One of the Bantu legends in my collection from Portuguese East Africa is probably of Semitic origin, and the song which it embodies seems also tinged with foreign color. Without doubt, Semitic tunes and musical intervals found their way to African ears, while, on the other side, African Negro drumbeats and syncopations must have influenced Berber, Moorish and thus perhaps even Spanish rhythms.[1]

[1]The following theory is advanced by Dr. W. E. B. DuBois, author of "The Souls of Black Folk," "The Negro," etc.:
"The Semites and black Africans are from one parent Asiatic stem, and ever since their prehistoric differentiation and separation there has been in historic times continual contact and intermingling in the North of Africa, around the Red Sea and down the coasts of the Indian Ocean. This was not merely the comparatively modern contact of Arab master and Negro slave, but an earlier and much more important contact of two systems of culture, Arabian and African. In the Sudan, in the mountains of Abyssinia, and in Mozambique, not only did Arabian culture penetrate Central Africa, but Negro culture changed and modified the African culture of the Semites, and especially in art and music and industry the African influence can be traced far into Spain and Arabia." (Cf. Frobenius, "Und Afrika Sprach.")

44

Another characteristic of the Negro, musically, is a harmonic sense indicating musical intuition of a high order. This instinct for natural polyphony is made clear in the recording of the Negro songs in this collection, wherein I have noted the four-part harmony as sung extemporaneously by colored boys who had had no musical training whatever. Some of the most beautiful improvisational part-singing that I ever heard arose from the throats of utterly illiterate black laborers in a tobacco factory. One has but to attend a colored church, whether North or South, to hear men and women break naturally into alto, tenor or bass parts (and even subdivisions of these), to realize how instinctively the Negro musical mind thinks harmonies. I have heard players in colored bands perform one part on an instrument and sing another while all those around him were playing and singing still different parts. Yet it has been asserted by some people that the harmonic sense of the Negro is a product of white environment and that the black man owes his intuitive gift to the slave-holders who sang hymns, ballads and popular songs in his hearing! With all due allowance for white influence, which has been great, of course, the fact remains that in savage Africa, remote from European culture, many of the most primitive pagan songs are sung in parts with elaborate interludes on drums tuned to different pitches. Indeed, the music of the Dark Continent is rich in polyphonic as well as rhythmic suggestions for the European. Perhaps the war may help to prick some of the vanity of the white race, which, looking down with self-assumed superiority upon other races, is quick to condemn delinquencies as native characteristics, and to ascribe to its own influences anything worthy; whereas the reverse is, alas, all too often the case. Certainly the art of Africa, of India, of the Orient and of North America owes to the Anglo-Saxon only corruption and commercialization. As for American Negro music, those songs that are most like the music of the white people—and they are not few—are the least interesting: they are sentimental, tame, and uneventful both in melody and rhythm. On the other hand, such melodies as "Go down, Moses," "Four and Twenty Elders on Their Knees," "Run, Mary, Run," these speak from the very soul of the black race, and no white man could have conceived them. They have a dignity barbaric, aloof and wholly individual which lifts them cloud-high above any "white" hymns that the Negro might have overheard. Austere as Egyptian bas-relief, simple as Congo sculpture, they are mighty melodies, and they are Negro.

So much, very briefly, for rhythmic, melodic and harmonic comparisons between American Negro and native African music. Now as to the form of the songs: The Negro Spirituals (prayer-songs) open with a choral refrain or burthen, followed by a freely declaimed extemporaneous verse or even just a few words of solo sung by a single voice. Then comes the chorus or burthen again; another verse or solo; again the chorus; more verses, and so on, indefinitely, until the song ends with the chorus—a rounded whole. Ballads and songs consisting of verses and choral refrains are of course common to Europeans and Americans. Yet the form of some of the African ceremonial and pagan religious songs (some of which I recorded) is in essence like that of the Spiritual, particularly in the declamatory and improvisational quality of its solo, sung by a priest or shaman while the chorus is chanted by a great circle of people. Whatever part white influence may have played in the development of the Spiritual in this country, it is certain that the choral form regularly alternating with the extemporaneous or sometimes traditional solo (or solo followed by a chorus) is an ancient art-expression of the black race in Africa.

As to the manner in which Negro folk-songs spring into being, in a little essay entitled "Negro Music at Birth"[1] I have tried to picture what I myself have witnessed of the spontaneous creation of Negro choral chants when a group of colored people, catching up a musical phrase sung by one person, improvised corresponding phrases till, carried away by the emotion of the moment and welded into one impulse by a common ecstasy, they shaped a song through unity of group sentiment in the same way that an individual composer, in improvising, builds up a composition on a given theme. Sometimes Negro chants grow from one another instead of from an original source, even as some plants bud from slips instead of from seeds. Often some singer has remembered a line or phrase from a previously heard religious song, and has flung this out in "meet'n' " to be seized by the rest of the congregation and moulded into a new song. Thus we often see the root-idea of one song flowering into different form in another; or sometimes we find whole borrowed phrases cropping out in songs otherwise unrelated. This is true of words as well as of musical ideas. And the words of Negro songs are often folk-poems of great intrinsic interest.

In any consideration of these poems, we should remember that part of their child-like and in a sense almost inarticulate quality is due not only to the child-spirit of the race, but also to the fact that, to the deported African in this country, English was a foreign tongue only the rudiments of which (and these often distorted) were mastered by the unlettered slave. Sometimes a sublime flash of imagery shines through a few poor words, crude and misshapen. Whereas in the songs of Africa, simple and child-like though many of them are, the idea suffers none of that lameness of expression that so often lends a note of unconscious and touching comedy to American Negro verse. Humor the Negro has in plenty—healthy and boisterous fun; but the humor of some of the texts is far from intentional. It is only owing to limited opportunity that so often the highest reaches of poetic imagination (common to the Negro, as to most simple people who live close to nature) had to be expressed in the very few every-day English words—and these in dialect—that formed the whole vocabulary of the slave-poet. However, this very poverty of means gave birth to a unique poetic quality, poignant with character, quaint and ingenuous; also it throws the imagery forth with striking simplicity and directness in verses like the following, breathing the exaltation of the mountains:

> Did yo' ever
> Stan' on mountun,
> Wash yo' han's
> In a cloud?

And this, born perhaps of a hidden religious meeting in the woods:

> Ma head got wet wid de midnight dew:
> Come along home to Jesus;
> De mo'nin' star was a witness, too:
> Come along home to Jesus.

[1]See Foreword, Book IV, this series.

With what few words, and yet how clear-drawn is the oft-recurring picture of Jesus riding as a conquering king[1] and even appearing intimately as a personal liberator:

> Massa Jesus, He come a-rid*in'* by
> An' bought my liberty.

Touchingly naïve is the imagery of the "Gospel-Train" speeding so fast to salvation when joyful voices eagerly call us to "git on board!" To the simple black man, as to the American Indian, railroads must have been not prosaic realities, but things of real wonder.[2] And then, with what simplicity is the glory of the saved soul expressed in many a Negro verse by the thought of radiance, as in the song "Ev'ry time I feel de Spirit," and:

> Oh, den ma little soul gwine t' shine—shine—
> Den ma little soul gwine t' shine along!

And again:

> I's got a mudder in de Hebb'n,
> Out*shine* de sun,
> Out*shine* de sun,
> Out*shine* de sun!
> I's got a mudder in de Hebb'n
> 'Way beyon' de moon!

As Negro song-poems are usually conceived in the minds of their creators simultaneously with the music, the words bear the rhythmic values of the musical phrases, giving us a characteristic Negro accentuation different from anything else in the English language. Therefore it has seemed to me appropriate here to draw attention to a possible wealth of inspiration in the rich variety of rhythmic effects offered by Negro verse, *scanned as sung*—a variety that might be adapted by poets even without the African's inversion of the natural rhythms of our tongue. So, in my transcription of the song-poems, I have reproduced the accents given by the singing in this collection, reaffirming that in Negro song *it is the music* which determines the rhythms of the phrase, rather than the words. Yet it must always be borne in mind that as no two singers will sing the music alike in all details, so probably no two song-poets will stress the verse in exactly the same way. For, as I have said elsewhere, "Freedom of complete individualism is the inalienable right of every Negro bard."

All who are familiar with Negro folk-songs know how the vowel "a" (pronounced "ah") often precedes a word or sometimes is added at the end, filling out a melodic phrase, intensifying a bit of rhythmic emphasis, or softening and binding together in that fluency demanded by the Negro ear the sterner syllables of the English tongue. The verses here recorded are offered in dialect in the belief that thus is best preserved the full individuality, the color and the unique racial charm of the old plantation folk-songs.

Though I have striven to set upon paper the characteristics of Negro singing, there are always sounds both in words and music that defy the pen. The mellow softness of pronunciation added to vocal peculiarities—the subtle embellishment of grace-notes, turns and quavers, and the delightful little upward break in the voice—these can be but crudely indicated or described in the hope of awakening true memory in those who know Negro song, or of appealing with some vividness to the imagination of others

[1]See "*O Ride on, Jesus.*" Book I of this series.   [2]See p. 72.

47

who must rely for their picture solely upon the printed page. A recorder realizes, perhaps better than can another, how approximate only is any notation of music that was never conceived by the singers as a written thing. When one rereads the fixed transcription it seems to bear the same relation to the fluent original that the peep of a caged canary does to the free caroling of a bird on open wing. Would that some genius would add to our system of notation a gamut of more delicate symbols that would enable us better to express the unconscious voices of true folk-singers.

Those of us who are now recording the old Negro melodies keenly realize that we come late to the harvesting, and that a generation and more have lived since the originators of the slave-songs passed from the plantations. Yet free Negroes still work in the fields of the Southland, singing the old songs, and the racial quality of Negro singing has not died. Changes may have occurred. But so strong is the individuality of Negro song that even in this latter day it yet presents unique characteristics wholly worthy of study and record.

We of the white race are at last awakening to the fact that the Negro in our midst stands at the gates of human culture with full hands, laden with gifts. Too long in this country have we barred the door. The war has driven home to us this truth: we no longer merely tolerate the presence of the black race, and with anxiety at that—we need the Negro, and he is here to stay. So hard would it be for our Southern States to progress industrially without their colored population that the country has witnessed the spectacle of State legislation enacted to keep the Negro from migrating to Northern fields of labor. Even as we now learn that the black man's contribution to the industrial development of our land is an essential economic factor, so we have but to unlock the gate to see that he can be equally important to cultural evolution in the "melting pot" of the United States, and that his presence among us may be a powerful stimulus to the art, music, letters and drama of the American Continent.

NATALIE CURTIS BURLIN.

'TIS ME, O LORD

The recording of this song is dedicated to the memory of the late

ROBERT CURTIS OGDEN

WHOSE NAME BELONGS INSEPARABLY TO THE QUICKENED CAUSE OF EDUCATION IN THE SOUTH. THOUGH WEIGHTED WITH THE CARES OF A LARGE BUSINESS, ROBERT ODGEN'S VISION SOUGHT THE NATION'S GOOD BY THE UPLIFT OF THE INDIVIDUAL THROUGH EDUCATION. FREELY HE GAVE OF TIME AND FORTUNE TO THE AWAKENING OF INTEREST IN THE PROBLEMS OF THE SOUTHLAND WHICH, STRICKEN BY THE CIVIL WAR, STILL STRUGGLES IN ITS ADVANCE AGAINST THE BACKWARD PULL OF ILLITERACY AMONG THE RURAL WHITE POPULATION AS AMONG THE BLACK. THE CONFERENCES FOR EDUCATION IN THE SOUTH TO WHICH MR. OGDEN YEARLY BROUGHT BY SPECIAL TRAIN GROUPS OF FAMOUS EDUCATORS AS HIS INVITED GUESTS, BECAME THROUGH HIS PERSONAL INFLUENCE A MEETING GROUND FOR THE GROWTH OF BETTER UNDERSTANDING BETWEEN SOUTH AND NORTH. INDEED, THE SOUTHERN EDUCATION BOARD AND THE GENERAL EDUCATION BOARD—BRANCHES OF A SOUNDLY ORGANIZED PROGRESSIVE MOVEMENT FOR THE BETTERMENT OF THE MASSES OF OUR PEOPLE—OWE AN INCALCULABLE DEBT IN THEIR INCEPTION AND SCOPE TO THE UNSELFISH DEDICATION OF THE GREAT-HEARTED MAN WHO IN EARLY LIFE HAD BEEN FIRED BY THE FRIENDSHIP AND THE IDEALS OF GENERAL ARMSTRONG, THE FOUNDER OF HAMPTON INSTITUTE. TO THE SUPPORT OF HAMPTON AND THE FURTHERING OF ITS AIMS MR. OGDEN GAVE HIMSELF WITH TIRELESS ENTHUSIASM. NOW, ON THE SCHOOL GROUNDS, THE OGDEN MEMORIAL BUILDING ENSHRINES THE THOUGHT OF A LIFELONG FRIEND. THOUSANDS OF BLACK BOYS AND GIRLS REMEMBER WITH GRATITUDE THE PRESIDENT OF HAMPTON'S BOARD OF TRUSTEES WHO PRESENTED TO THEM THEIR DIPLOMAS ON GRADUATION FROM THE INSTITUTE. AND AS THESE STREAMS OF YOUNG PEOPLE WENT FORTH FROM HAMPTON TO BRING LIGHT TO THEIR RACE, THEY CARRIED WITH THEM AS POSSESSIONS NOT LESS PRECIOUS THAN THEIR WRITTEN CERTIFICATES THOSE WORDS OF COUNSEL AND CHEER WHICH MADE THE VOICE OF ROBERT OGDEN A PERSONAL APPEAL TO THE HEARTS OF HUMBLE WORKERS, AS IT WAS A GUIDING INSPIRATION TO THE MINDS OF MANY OF THE GREATEST EDUCATORS IN THE UNITED STATES.

'TIS ME, O LORD

Recorded from the singing of

Ira Godwin	("Lead")	Agriculture;	Virginia
Joseph Barnes	(Tenor)	Tinsmith;	"
William Cooper	(Baritone)	Schoolteacher;	"
Timothy Carper	(Bass)	Bricklayer;	"

The problem of inter-racial adjustment, involving the need of a cordial mutual understanding between the widely differing races of the United States, is admittedly one of the greatest issues of American life. No one man has perhaps done more to help solve that problem than General Samuel Chapman Armstrong, founder of Hampton Normal and Agricultural Institute at Hampton, Virginia. The pioneer industrial school for Negroes and Indians in this country, Hampton now numbers about nine hundred students annually, most famous of whom was Booker T. Washington, the founder of Tuskegee Institute in Alabama.[1]

"Learning by doing"—this is one of the precepts of Hampton Institute. Not only have most of the buildings on the school grounds been reared by student labor, but some of them have been "sung up," as they say at Hampton, through the proceeds of folk-song concerts given for the benefit of the school. Every phase of the life at Hampton has the vital coöperation of the black boys and girls who are formed by it and who in turn help to shape it. Not only does folk-song throb in the very arteries of the institution, but it has gone out from Hampton as a race expression to make friends for the Negro and to raise money for his education. Meetings in behalf of the school are held all over the country, in halls, theatres, drawing-rooms and in the open air, where race questions are discussed and the purpose of the industrial training school explained. Always at these gatherings a quartet of colored boys sings the old melodies. These slave-songs, speaking as they do of the patience, loyalty and long endurance of the race which the white man first brought here for gainful ends, make their own unconscious appeal for justice and help in the upward struggle of the freedman.

There are several self-organized and self-trained quartets at Hampton. Each year the best voices are chosen by the school to sing Hampton's message far abroad during the vacation months. The boys meet and practice together during off hours in the school term preparatory to going forth in what they call the "Hampton campaign." It is the singing of the quartet for the summer of 1915 that is here recorded. Each afternoon during the month of May I used to attend the practice meetings of these four boys, who improvised the harmonies of the songs, some of which were partly traditional at the school, while others were individual to this particular group. All four voices were peculiarly beautiful and absolutely untrained. Sensuously musical they were in timbre—mellow, full and reed-like, touched by that elemental emotional quality that makes the slave-songs, when sung by Negroes, so full of simple pathos. Yet a sunny happiness and infectious good-humor pervaded the

[1]See pp. v, 3 and 13.

personality of these boys, and I cannot say enough for the patience and the enthusiastic coöperation with which they helped me to note accurately their singing of the songs of their race. This old spiritual, " 'Tis me, O Lord," was first heard in Alabama by Robert Moton,[1] formerly the colored commandant at Hampton, and now principal at Tuskegee Institute. He caught the melody at once by ear and brought it back to Hampton, where it was extemporaneously harmonized by the students and speedily absorbed into the life of the school. Its devout, simple humility, expressing a depth of religious feeling, makes one see, through music, a soul on its knees.

'TIS ME, O LORD

'Tis me, 'tis me, O Lord,
   Standin' in de need of prayer—
      O Lord!
'Tis me, 'tis me, O Lord,
   Standin' in de need of prayer.

'Tis not my Mudder but it's me, O Lord,
   Standin' in de need of prayer—
      O Lord!
'Tis not my Mudder but it's me, O Lord,
   Standin' in de need of prayer.

'Tis me, 'tis me, O Lord,
   Standin' in de need of prayer—
      O Lord!
'Tis me, 'tis me, O Lord,
   Standin' in de need of prayer.

'Tis not my Sister but it's me, O Lord,
   Standin' in de need of prayer—
      O Lord!
'Tis not my Sister but it's me, O Lord,
   Standin' in de need of prayer.

'Tis me, 'tis me, O Lord,
   Standin' in de need of prayer—
      O Lord!
'Tis me, 'tis me, O Lord,
   Standin' in de need of prayer.

[1]See p. 32.

'Tis me, O Lord

Recorded
and transcribed by
Natalie Curtis-Burlin

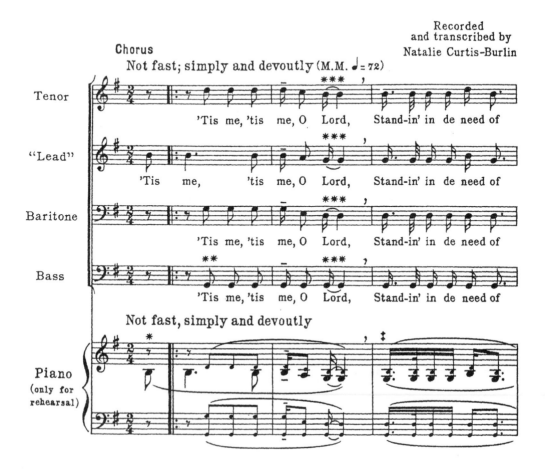

Chorus

Not fast; simply and devoutly (M.M. ♩ = 72)

Tenor: 'Tis me, 'tis me, O Lord, Stand-in' in de need of

"Lead": 'Tis me, 'tis me, O Lord, Stand-in' in de need of

Baritone: 'Tis me, 'tis me, O Lord, Stand-in' in de need of

Bass: 'Tis me, 'tis me, O Lord, Stand-in' in de need of

Piano (only for rehearsal): Not fast, simply and devoutly

* The melody is carried in the voice of the "Lead" or Leader printed in the piano-part in large type. It must sound above the other voices.

** Sometimes this variant of the Bass part is sung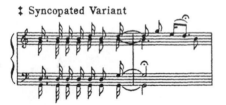
'Tis me, 'tis me, O Lord

*** On all notes marked with *** there is a slight drawing out of the rhythm, though not sufficient to warrant a fermata sign (⌢). It is so natural and appropriate to prolong these notes (and chords) in a prayer-song that the listener is hardly conscious of a pause, though it is very apparent with the metronome. The slight holding back of these notes must not be so marked as to interrupt the steady rhythmic onward beat of the song.

‡ Syncopated Variant

See three ✱✱✱, previous page.

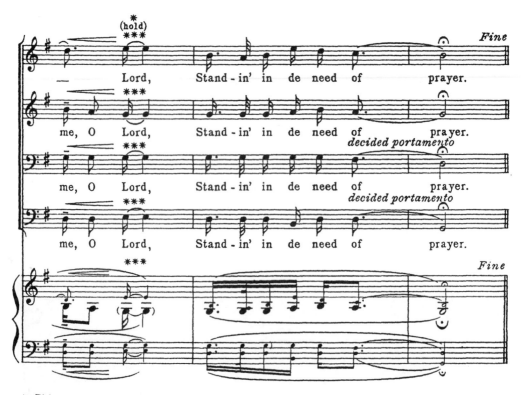

* This note, marking the climax of the phrase, is held the longest of all.

Verse 1

Stand-in' in de need of

very legato

'Tis not ma Mud-der, but it's me, O Lord, Stand-in' in de need of

Stand-in' in de need of

Stand-in' in de need of

prayer; 'Tis not ma Mud-der, but it's me, O Lord, Stand-in' in de need of

prayer; 'Tis not ma Mud-der, but it's me, O Lord, Stand-in' in de need of

decided portamento

prayer; 'Tis not ma Mud-der, but it's me, O Lord, Stand-in' in de need of

prayer; 'Tis not ma Mud-der, but it's me, O Lord, Stand-in' in de need of

Variant   Lead

*   **

Bass

Sometimes the Bass singer per-
forms this characteristic bit of an-
ticipative syncopation.

55

This song may be continued indefinitely by adding new verses in which the words Fader, Brudder, Deacon, Preacher, or any other term of human relationship may be substituted for the words Mudder and Sister.

LISTEN TO DE LAMBS

To my friend

GEORGE FOSTER PEABODY

humanitarian and true Christian, the recording of this song is dedicated.

As trustee of Hampton Institute since 1884 and also of its Investment Committee, Mr. Peabody has constantly labored to widen the influence of Hampton, and at the same time, as a native of Georgia, he has emphasized the Southern sympathy with the cause of Negro education which throughout the country has long known his substantial help. In the South as well as in the North he is consequently both honored and loved. Together with Mr. Ogden he helped to found both the Southern Conferences for Education and the Southern Education Board; and as Treasurer, for a time, of the General Education Board and of the Jeanes Foundation for the Benefit of Rural Schools, his business training and counsel materially advanced the growth of these organizations. A champion of radical political democracy and of that democracy of the spirit that cannot rest at ease while those less fortunate must suffer for lack of opportunity, Mr. Peabody felt obligated to devote to the public good the bulk of his accumulations and therefore he retired from business in order that he might give all his energies to the wide promotion of human welfare, both in large organized movements and in that discerning and thoughtful interest in individuals which has made his work for others a nobly personal gift. Many black men, as well as white, proudly count him as their friend, and all are as grateful for his unfailing advice and encouragement as for his material aid.

LISTEN TO DE LAMBS

Recorded from the singing of

Ira Godwin	("Lead")	Agriculture;	Virginia
Joseph Barnes	(Tenor)	Tinsmith;	"
William Cooper	(Baritone)	Schoolteacher;	"
Timothy Carper	(Bass)	Bricklayer;	"

This Spiritual is filled with rare imaginative quality in word and music. A previous notation places it in D minor and in regular $\frac{4}{4}$ rhythm.[1] It is possible that through long usage the wide emotional latitude of the freer rhythm which I have recorded has grown traditional; yet it is hard now to

---

[1] "Religious Folk-Songs of the Negro" (Hampton Institute Press).

57

tell whether the D minor version noted many years ago adhered more or less to a Negro rendering, or is something of an adaptation. In writing down Negro songs most white people have caught the melody by ear and then added harmonies of their own. Yet often even the melody has not closely followed the characteristic details of Negro rhythm, nor the free extemporaneous quality of Negro singing. The song has consciously been reduced to what the recording musician thinks *should* be its correct form, so that the transcription does not really represent a song as the Negroes sing it, but a musical translation. It is noted, not as it is, but as the recorder thinks it should be, or else it is simply used as a theme for the creation of a new composition— which is quite another, though wholly legitimate field.

In "Listen to de Lambs" it seems to me that the pentatonic character of most Negro melodies would point to F major as well as D minor as a natural harmonization of the opening phrase; and I am inclined to think that both harmonizations must always have been in general use among Negroes. But, in the version which I have recorded, the chromatics in the next phrase *"all a-cryin'"* are undoubtedly comparatively modern, although they possess keen emotional quality and were invented years ago by the Negroes themselves, who have made this harmonization traditional at Hampton. Perhaps some older version sustained the tonic chord throughout the first bars until the striking diatonic major progression upward, in consecutive fifths and octaves, lifted the first part of the song to its climax. Further study in the South may bring forth many other versions differing both melodically and harmonically, for the Negroes say: "We don't know just how we sing till you ask us. We just sing the way we *feel!*" Where music is "felt" in intuitive harmonies, where its very nature is spontaneous and creative, who shall say whether or not a given rendering of a traditional song is *"correct"!* All I have tried to do is to record with entire accuracy this single beautiful version —to put on paper at least one faithful reproduction of the fluent loveliness of Negro singing. If another group of Southern Negroes from another state should sing the same song quite differently, no doubt it might be just as authoritative and quite as interesting.

Though I have tried to write these songs in truth to the sound and sense of the Negroes' own singing, it is to be hoped that the colored people in the large towns, who have forgotten the old songs, will seek to cherish their own innate gift for improvisational singing rather than slavishly to follow this or any other notation. For the living inspirational faculty, so rare indeed, should be to them of greater value than any crystallization; although for the world of music at large, careful records of the old traditional singing must be made and preserved. In this recording, I have sought to indicate through expression marks the ingenuous depth of feeling with which the Negroes sing this song. It would be unfortunate, however, if these efforts to express Negro sentiment should be misread into over-elaborate self-consciousness or sentimentality. To avoid any such danger, a brief description of the effect produced by the Negro singers may not be amiss.

The song opens slowly and softly, with a certain weirdness of atmosphere, suggesting a mental picture of the "Lambs," the weak and poor of the earth, craving the Good Shepherd, huddling gently together, "all a-cryin',"—crying for the promised release: *"I want t' go t' Hebb'n when I die."* Then comes a jubilant summons full of hope—"Come on, sister, wid yo' ups and downs"; and the cry "Want t' go t' Hebb'n when I die" takes on quick courage and appeal.

Yet more tenderly sounds the promise, "Angels wait'n' fo' t' give you crown," and this is followed by a touching confidence when the refrain is again firmly repeated: "Want t' go t' Hebb'n when I die." Like many of the Spirituals of slave times, this song dwells on the imminence of the next world. Of course, the effect described is not thought out or consciously achieved by the singer—it is entirely emotional. For the Negroes always explain: "We sing the way we *feel*."

Mention should here be made of a Negro choral work by R. Nathaniel Dett, a colored musician whose composition, based on this Spiritual, is designed as a somewhat elaborate development of the original Negro theme and is intended primarily for use as a church anthem. It is to be hoped that Mr. Dett's effort may help to lead the educated members of the Negro race back to the old songs from which they have turned away. For the Spirituals, *just as they stand in all their primitive simplicity*, are of monumental beauty and have their rightful place in musical art.—See "Listen to de Lambs," by R. Nathaniel Dett (G. Schirmer, publisher).

LISTEN TO DE LAMBS

O Listen to de Lambs
      All a-cryin',
Listen to de Lambs
      All a-cryin',
Listen to de Lambs
      All a-cryin',
I want t' go t' Hebb'n[1] when I die!

Come on,[2] Sister, wid' yo' ups an' downs,
      Want t' go t' Hebb'n when I die;
Angels wait'n' fo' t' give you crown,
      Want t' go t' Hebb'n when I die.

O Listen to de Lambs
      All a-cryin',
Listen to de Lambs
      All a-cryin',
Listen to de Lambs
      All a-cryin',
I want t' go t' Hebb'n when I die!

[1]The word "Hebb'n" in Negro dialect has a soft sound made by closing the lips on the "*b*" and sounding the "*n*" with the mouth shut. This gives to the consonant "*b*" an intermediary sound between "*b*" and "*v*."

[2]The "*o*" in the word "*on*" is pronounced with a long *o* in Negro dialect, thus: "ōn" (or "ohn").

Come on, Sister, an' a-don't be 'shame',
Want t' go t' Hebb'n when I die;
Angels wait'n' t' write yo' name.
Want t' go t' Hebb'n when I die.

O Listen to de Lambs
               All a-cryin',
Listen to de Lambs
               All a-cryin',
Listen to de Lambs
               All a-cryin';
I want t' go t' Hebb'n when I die!

This song may be continued indefinitely by adding new verses in which the words "Fader," "Brudder," "Deacon," "Preacher" or any other term of relationship may be substituted for "Mudder" and "Sister."—See p. 4.

Listen to de Lambs

* The students at Hampton often sing this song a whole tone higher than it is here recorded, the Negro Tenor attacking high B flat with ease and beauty. It has been thought wiser, however, to place the song more fully within the range of average voices.

** The voice of the "Lead" (or Leader) carries the melody and is printed in the piano-part in large type. It must sound above the other voices.

*** This phrase is really sung throughout thus:

When the chorus is sung for the last time a slight pause is made after the word "Heav'n," thus:

* The "o" in the word <u>on</u> is pronounced very long in Negro dialect, thus: "ōn" or "ohn."
A third verse, seldom, if ever, sung at Hampton, bears the following words: "Mind out, brudder, how you walk de cross, want t' go t' Heav'n when I die, foot might slip an' yo' soul get lost, want t', etc."

O EV'RY TIME I FEEL DE SPIRIT

The record of this song is affectionately dedicated to

DAVID MANNES

ARTIST AND TEACHER

WHOSE WHOLE CAREER HAS BEEN CONSECRATED TO THE LINKING
OF ART WITH LIFE.

ON a May evening in Virginia, at the Commencement Exercises of Hampton Institute, when the graduating class of colored students was seated on the platform and tier upon tier of eager black faces rose almost to the very ceiling, someone told this story:

"There was once a Negro musician named Douglas who, during the days of slavery, had somehow made his way to Europe, where he met with no race-prejudice and became an excellent violinist. After the civil war and the emancipation of the slaves, Douglas returned to the United States, the home of all his relatives, believing that now the Negroes were indeed free. But because of his color he found every door still barred; no orchestra would admit him; in the field of serious music there was then no place for the Negro.

"Passing through the streets of New York one day the broken-hearted artist heard the tones of a violin floating out from a basement window; he listened: evidently it was a child's hand that drew the bow. Irresistibly impelled, he entered the basement dwelling, and there found a little white boy playing on a crude, cheap violin. On questioning the mother the Negro found that she had no means to gratify the child's passion for music. 'Then let me teach him!' Douglas said. And so into the soul of this little white boy, denied all opportunity, the colored musician, equally denied, poured all that he had learned. 'For he is white,' thought Douglas, 'and will do what I can never do because I am black.'

"And now," continued the Hampton narrator, "comes the sequel of that story which happened a long time ago, for that little white boy, whose first lessons were from a Negro, is now one of America's best-known artists, who has come to Hampton and will play for us to-night."

Then onto the platform, violin in hand, stepped David Mannes. Forgetful of the audience he turned and faced the colored students, playing only to them; and in this instinctive act it seemed as though the violinist strove to give to the Negro race what the black musician had given him. And it was in direct outcome of that memorable evening in Virginia that a year later, in New York, with Hampton's help, the Music School Settlement for Colored People was founded, with David Mannes as associate director and inspiring friend to the faculty of colored teachers.

May the spirit of human reciprocity, the linking sense of inter-racial indebtedness that prompted the founding of that school, spread to other fields of mutual recognition between white men and black.

O EV'RY TIME I FEEL DE SPIRIT

Recorded from the singing of

Ira Godwin	("Lead")	Agriculture;	Virginia
Joseph Barnes	(Tenor)	Tinsmith;	"
William Cooper	(Baritone)	Schoolteacher;	"
Timothy Carper	(Bass)	Bricklayer;	"

Of all the Spirituals, this is one of the most touching in its prayerful suggestion and quiet reverence, and in the poetic imagery of its verse, couched in a few crude words, elemental in their simplicity, yet somehow conveying the grandeur of the vision of God on the mountain-top and the dazed soul beholding heaven in wonder.

O ev'ry time I feel[1] de Spirit
  Movin' in ma heart—I pray,
O ev'ry time I feel de Spirit
  Movin' in ma heart—I pray.

Upon de mountun ma Lord spoke,
Out of his mouth came fi-er an' smoke.

O ev'ry time I feel de Spirit
  Movin' in ma heart—I pray,
O ev'ry time I feel de Spirit
  Movin' in ma heart—I pray.

Jordan[2] Ribber chilly an' col',
Chill de body, but not de soul.

O ev'ry time I feel de Spirit
  Movin' in ma heart—I pray,
O ev'ry time I feel de Spirit
  Movin' in ma heart—I pray.

All aroun' me looks so shine.
Ask ma Lord if all was mine.

O ev'ry time I feel de Spirit
  Movin' in ma heart—I pray,
O ev'ry time I feel de Spirit
  Movin' in ma heart—I pray.

[1] The more primitive Negroes of St. Helena Island sing "feels."
[2] Pronounced "*Jerdan.*"

O ev'ry time I feel de Spirit

Sung with simplicity, breadth and reverence. An even, legato tone throughout

* The voice of the "Lead" (or leader) carries the melody of the song and is printed in the piano accompaniment in large type. It must sound above the other voices.

** Sung sometimes

*** The pause here equals a half-note, thus:

**** The pause here usually equals a quarter-note, thus:

* Whenever this phrase occurs in the many repetitions of the"Chorus," it may be sung as here recorded, or as recorded on first page, the two versions being interchangeable at will. Or, one voice
may sing the phrase broken by a rest, as above, while the other voices sing legato, or vice-versa.
The singing is extemporaneous, and the individual singers breathe when they like, breaking a
phrase whenever they choose.
** Pause as before. *** When the"chorus" is sung for the last time there is a long pause on
the final word "pray."
**** The "o" in the word on is pronounced very long in Negro dialect, thus: "ōn" or "ohn".

67

* Pronounced "fi-er," two syllables.   ** Pronounced "Jerdan."
Note: Among the primitive Negroes of South Carolina the choral refrain is sung "feels de Spirit."

GOD'S A-GWINE TER MOVE ALL DE TROUBLES AWAY

TO PERCY GRAINGER

(who loves this song)

COMPOSER, PIANIST, FOLK-LORIST

THIS RECORD IS DEDICATED WITH WARM APPRECIATION OF THOSE QUALITIES OF ARTISTIC INSIGHT AND HUMAN SYMPATHY THAT MAKE HIM A FIRM FRIEND OF THE NEGRO AND OF NEGRO MUSIC; FOR THE UNCONSCIOUS ART OF SIMPLE MEN FINDS REVERENT RECOGNITION AND BUOYANT RESPONSE FROM THE GENIUS WHOSE OWN SUNNY NATURE MAKES ALL WHO KNOW HIM BELIEVE THAT

"GOD'S A-GWINE TER MOVE ALL DE TROUBLES AWAY."

ONE night in New York, under the auspices of the Musical School Settlement for Colored People, a concert of Negro music performed by colored musicians was given in Carnegie Hall. Among the listeners, spellbound with interest, sat Percy Grainger. A talented young colored pianist was playing for the first time before a great audience. Trembling with nervousness, her fingers missed the notes, her mind grew blank, and suddenly she dropped her face in her hands. Then pulling herself together, she somehow finished her piece and left the piano. Meanwhile Percy Grainger had disappeared. Hurrying behind the scenes he met the dejected little pianist as she came from the stage. "Don't mind," he said comfortingly, "we have all done the same thing; every artist has. That's part of a public career. Go back and play again. Don't you hear them applauding? This time you'll play better than ever!" Thus encouraged, the girl reappeared before her audience and now came off with flying colors. She had never met the great pianist before, but he marked a turning-point in her life, for he had helped her to change failure to victory. And this little incident seemed a symbol of Grainger's influence in all his generous contact with the "disadvantaged people" and with the struggling artists of the Negro race.

GOD'S A-GWINE TER MOVE ALL DE TROUBLES AWAY

Recorded from the singing of

Charles H. Tynes	("Lead")
Freeman W. Crawley	(Tenor)
Samuel E. Phillips	(Baritone)
John H. Wainwright	(Bass)

The above group of singers is the oldest quartet at Hampton, some of the members having graduated from the school over thirty years ago. Though none of them have had technical musical training, all are musicians by the grace of God and have sung together for so long that the blending interplay of their voices has attained rare artistic perfection. At the Panama-Pacific International Exposition, where they sang all summer at the Educational Exhibit, they were awarded a medal.[1]

In this song the "lead" is, of course, free to sing the narrative verses as he pleases, although retaining the same general melodic outline which conforms to the thematic pattern of the song.

It is of peculiar interest to see how the singer here recorded (Tynes) has adapted, with unerring dramatic sense, his musical déclamation to the natural flow of the words—an ideal consciously sought by great composers and here unconsciously attained without any sacrifice of the charming folk-song melody, and with a naïveté and simplicity altogether delightful. The emphasis of the triplets in the description of Samson as "de stronges' man ever walked on earth":

De strong-es' man__ ev-er walked on earth

and the awesome age of Methusaleh depicted with such an expressive *portamento:*

Me-thū-sa-leh was__ de old-es' man

these are flashes of real descriptive talent, not less great because intuitive merely.

The humming accompaniment of the other singers forms a swinging background to the melody. "We jes' foller the 'lead'," the singers explain. "When he goes up, we go up too. No, of course, we don't know jes' what he's goin' t' do—we jes' *feel* it, an' we sing like he sings—that's all." However, in noting this "following," I find that although the "feel" was that all voices moved together, the "lead" was naturally sometimes a little ahead. I have therefore sought to retain this inspirational quality by writing down in detail what the singers actually did—not the theory of the thing, but the practice—although of course they do not always do the same thing, and another "lead" presenting a different musical interpretation of the narrative phrases will have to be followed according to his own version. Such individual changes apply chiefly to the rhythm, although the "lead" may always make alterations in the less important notes of the melody.

As regards white singers: If in the narrative the syncopation (the slight lagging behind of the accompanying voices) might present rhythmic difficulties too subtle for average amateurs, it can be simplified by allowing the voices to follow the rhythm of the "lead" more closely. The singing must sound *"nat'cherl";* if the syncopations are laboriously learned they may be "jerky"; whereas the song as sung by Negroes has a lilt, a rolling swing that seems a part of the unconscious and pervading rhythms of nature. Besides

[1]See p. 5.

its humor, the refrain of the song is filled with a joyousness of faith and a devotional buoyancy that ought to put sun and courage into the heaviest heart and lift the most despairing spirit.

"God's a-gwine ter move all de troubles away," though native to Virginia, came to me from St. Helena Island,[1] off the coast of South Carolina, where the Negro population far outnumbers the white, and life in the cottonfields is still primitive and full of song. To the unlettered black man the Bible was an oral book and the familiar figures of Scripture were made to live through the eloquence of the colored preacher. Even as all Christian nations have lovingly absorbed the Bible personages and pictured them as belonging to their own people and time, so the same naïve race-appropriation that painted Italian, German and Flemish Virgins, now gives us, in this Negro song, a black Samson whose tight-curling hair must be "shaved as clean as yo' han'." Indeed, the reality of the Bible-heroes to the untutored slave can scarcely be more vividly and dramatically exemplified than in this old "Spiritual."

So far as I can find out, this song has never before been written down in any form; though to a totally different tune and another refrain, verses parallel in meaning are contained in a song from Miss Emily Halowell's able collection for Calhoun School: "Wasn't thet a witness fo' ma Lord."[2]

GOD'S A-GWINE TER MOVE ALL DE TROUBLES AWAY

God's[3] a-gwine ter move all de troubles away,
God's a-gwine ter move all de troubles away,
God's a-gwine ter move all de troubles away,
    See 'm no more till de comin' day!

Genesis, you understan',
Methusaleh was de oldes' man,
His age was nine hundred an' sixty-nine,
He died and went to Heaven in due time.

For God's a-gwine ter move all de troubles away,
God's a-gwine ter move all de troubles away,
God's a-gwine ter move all de troubles away,
    See 'm no more till de comin' day!

Dere was a man of de Pharisee,
His name was Nicodemus an' he wouldn't believe.
De same he came to Christ by night,
Want-a be taught out o' human sight.
Nicodemus was a man who wanted to know,
"Can a man be born-a when-a he is ol'?"
Christ tol' Nicodemus as a frien',
"A-man, you must be born again!"

[1] On this island is situated the Penn Industrial School, an outgrowth of Hampton Institute. (See p. 4, Book I, of this series).
[2] See "Calhoun Plantation Songs," by Emily Halowell (C. W. Thompson & Co., Boston, Mass.).
[3] Pronounced "Gawd."

For God's a-gwine ter move all de troubles away,
  God's a-gwine ter move all de troubles away,
  God's a-gwine ter move all de troubles away,
    See 'm no more till de comin' day!

a-Read about Samson from his birth,
De stronges' man ever walked on earth.
a-Read way back in de ancient time
He slew ten thousan' Philistine.
a-Samson he went a-walkin' about,
a-Samson's strength-a was never found out
Twell[1] his wife sat down upon his knee,
An'-a "Tell me whar yo' strength-a lies, ef you please."

a-Samson's wife she done talk so fair,
a-Samson tol' her "Cut off-a ma hair,
Ef you shave ma head jes' as clean as yo' han',
Ma strength-a will become-a like a natcherl man!"

For God's a-gwine ter move all de troubles away,
  God's a-gwine ter move all de troubles away,
  God's a-gwine ter move all de troubles away,
    See 'm no more till de comin' day!

The following additional verses were given to me by J. E. Blanton of Penn School, St. Helena Island.

There is a road to heaven laid,
By heavenly Truth the rails are made;
God's word the power, Truth the steam
That drives the engine of the train;
The Bible is the engineer
That points out the way to Heaven clear.

Now, poor sinner, is your time,
The Gospel[2] train is on the line;

.   .   .   .

Get yo' ticket 'fore yo' lef' behin'!

[1]Until, or till.

[2]Pronounced "Gawspel."

*God's a-gwine ter move all de troubles away

With slow and swinging rhythm (M.M. ♩ =80)

Chorus *Sung through twice after each verse, and at the opening of the song.*

Tenor: God's a-gwine ter move all de trou-bles a-way,—

** "Lead": God's a-gwine ter move all de trou-bles a-way,—

Baritone: God's gwine ter move all de trou-bles a-way,—

Bass: God's gwine ter move all de trou-bles a-way,—

With slow and swinging rhythm

Piano (only for rehearsal)

God's a-gwine ter move all de trou-bles a-way,— For

God's a-gwine ter move all de trou-bles a-way,— For

God's gwine ter move all de trou-bles a-way,— For

God's gwine ter move all de trou-bles a-way,— For

* Pronounced "Gawd."

** The voice of the "Lead" (or Leader) carries the melody and is printed in the piano-part in large type. It must sound above the other voices.

*** Variant:

73

God's a-gwine ter move all de trou-bles a-way,___ See 'm no more till de com-in' day. For com-in' day.___

Variant

walked on earth; a - Read way back in de an-cient time,— He slew ten thou-san'

Phi-lis-tines. A-Sam-son he went a-walk-in' a-bout, a - Sam-son's strength-a was

nev-er found out Twell his wife set down up - on his knee_ an' a

"Tell me whar yo' strength-a lies, ef you please." A - Sam-son's wife_ she done

* "Twell"_ until or till.

talk so fair,— a-Sam-son tol'— her, "Cut off-a ma hair, Ef you shave ma head_ jes'es

clean as yo' han', Ma strength-a will be-come-a like a nat-cherl man." For

forte

f

Chorus *D.C.*

For

For

For

Chorus *D.C.*

At the last repetition, the chorus is sung *pp*, with a long pause at the end.

81

BOOK III

WORK- and PLAY-SONGS

To
CORA M. FOLSON

Friend of Negroes and Indians,
Student of folk-lore and guardian of the folk-lore spirit at Hampton,
these recordings of Work- and Play-Songs are affectionately dedicated

Foreword   85   /   "Cotton in Song"   87

Cott'n-Pickin' Song

Notes   89   /   Music   93

Cott'n-Dance Song

Notes   98   /   Music   102

Cott'n-Packin' Song

Notes   107   /   Music   110

Corn-Shuckin' Song

Notes   111   /   Music   114

FOREWORD

"Who trains the chorus? It is marvelous!"

The question was eagerly put by a young German musician who was visiting the Hampton Institute in Virginia and for the first time heard the great chorus of nine hundred colored students sing the "Plantations," as the Negroes call the old melodies that had their birth in days of slavery—religious songs that were the voice of the bondsman's soul. From a technical as well as purely musical standpoint the extraordinary unity, the precision in "attack" and the faultless pitch of the Negro singers impelled the musician's query.

And my answer baffled him: "Why, no one trains these Negro boys and girls, their singing is natural."

"I don't mean," he persisted, "who trains their *voices* (of course, I understand that these are natural voices), but who teaches them their *parts:* soprano, alto, tenor, bass—who drills them as a chorus?"

"No one."

He stared at me incredulously. But I assured him that these black singers made up the "parts" themselves extemporaneously and sang together with the same spontaneity of unity that individuals feel when gathering with a group—they fall in line, and keep step as they walk. This quick contagion of musical sympathy, this instant amalgamation of the personal musical consciousness into a strong mass-feeling—this it is that would make any perfunctory "chorus-drilling" certain death to the inspirational spirit of those superbly simple old Negro songs.

But the musician would not believe that such results could be achieved by instinct alone. And so I finally referred him to "Major" Moton, now Booker Washington's successor as principal at Tuskeegee, who was at that time commandant at Hampton, and sang the solo parts—the "Lead" (leader), in Negro musical parlance. His reply emphasized through its laughing surprise the inborn, intuitive quality of the Negro's love for music:

"Why, *nobody* ever taught us to sing!"

"Well then, how do you do it?" asked the musician in amazement.

"I don't know. We *just sing*—that's all!"

Surely a people who can "just sing" in extemporaneous four- and six- and eight-part harmonies are gifted not only with rare melodic and rhythmic sense, but also with a natural talent for harmony that distinguishes the black race as among the most musically endowed of peoples.

The nine hundred boys and girls at Hampton whose chorus singing is so "marvelous" are not divided and seated according to "parts" like the usual white chorus. Indeed, technically speaking, this is no "chorus" at all—only a group of students at the Hampton Institute who sing because music is a part of their very souls. And so in chapel, where the old "plantations" are sung, the boys sit together at the sides, and the girls sit together in the middle, each singing any part that happens to lie easily within the range of his of her voice, harmonizing the slave-songs as they sing. A first alto may be wedged between two sopranos with a second alto directly in front of her. A boy singing high tenor may have a second tenor on one side of him and a second bass on the other. But the wonderful inspirational singing of this great choir is sustained without a flaw or a single deviation in pitch through song after song, absolutely without accompaniment.

"How do they do it?" One may well ask! For the singing is not only faultless in its simple and natural beauty, but profoundly stirring in its emotional wealth of feeling. ·Few listeners can withhold a catch in the throat when, after the final benediction in chapel, a deep silence which seems to hover like a benediction itself over those hundreds of bowed heads, is broken by a soft-breathed note of music, almost inaudible at first, like hushed wings, like the descent of the Holy Spirit. And then, still breathed rather than sung, gathering in volume as group after group catches it up, from those bent black heads rises a chanted "Amen" of such penetrating sweetness, such prayerful intensity, that—well, every white person that I have ever seen visit Hampton for the first time leaves chapel wiping his eyes!

"Only in Russia," declared one musician, "have I heard chorus singing comparable to this." Indeed, in my opinion, at Hampton and Tuskeegee Institutes, Fisk, and other Southern schools, are to be found the great folk-choruses of America.

Through the Negro this country is vocal with a folk-music intimate, complete and beautiful. Not that this is our only folk-lore, for the song of the American Indian is a unique contribution to the music of the world; also our Anglo-Saxon progenitors brought with them the songs and ballads of the British Isles, still held in purity in the mountain fastnesses of the Southern States, though strange versions of them crop up in the cowboy songs of the frontier. But it is the Negro music with its by-product of "Ragtime" that to-day most widely influences the popular song-life of America, and Negro rhythms have indeed captivated the world at large.[1] Nor may we foretell the impress that the voice of the slave will leave upon the Art of the country—a poetic justice, this! For the Negro, everywhere discriminated against, segregated and shunned, mobbed and murdered—he it is whose melodies are on all our lips, and whose rhythms impel our marching feet in a "war for democracy." The irresistible music that wells up from this sunny and un-resentful people is hummed and whistled, danced to and marched to, laughed over and wept over, by high and low and rich and poor throughout the land. The downtrodden black man whose patient religious faith has kept his heart still unembittered, is fast becoming the singing voice of all America. And in his song we hear a prophecy of the dignity and worth of Negro genius.

---

[1] Some have denied that our popular American music of to-day owes its stimulus to the Negro. A most interesting and conclusive account of the evolution of "Ragtime" is contained in the "Autobiography of an Ex-Colored Man" by James Weldon Johnson, published by Sherman French & Co., Boston. "Ragtime" is not unjustly condemned by many for the vulgarity of its first associations, a vulgarity that cannot be too deeply deplored, but which is fortunately fast slipping out of the march and dance songs of to-day. Yet this first association can not annihilate the interest of the Negro rhythmic form from which sprang "Ragtime," for this form has intrinsic character. Though now widely copied and almost mechanically manufactured by commercial white song-writers of cheap and "catchy" music, the extraordinary syncopation of ragtime, which makes the rhythm so compelling, is undoubtedly Negro and of real value and interest musically. Nor is this rhythmic peculiarty confined, with the Negro, to popular and secular music only. Lifted into noble breadth of accent, syncopation is found in the old Spirituals, or prayer-songs, for it is the rhythm natural to the Negro: intensely racial, its counterpart may be found in the native African songs from the Dark Continent. See Foreword to "Negro Folk-Songs," Book II, this series, p. 43.

COTTON IN SONG

Give us, oh, give us, the man who sings at his work! Be his occupation what it may, he is equal to any of those who follow the same pursuit in silent sullenness. He does more in the same time—he will do it better—he will persevere longer.

CARLYLE.

Song lightens labor all over the world, and in no country more so, perhaps, than in Africa, where music is a part of the very life of the natives, in whom the sense of rhythm is so highly developed that to rhythmize toil, through the regular cadences of chanted song, is to make it at once more natural as well as more effective. Many are the work-songs of the American Negro in the United States, songs improvised or made up on the spot to fit the task, and songs traditional. So well recognized is the fact that the Negro labors best when he labors with song, that in old days a man who could lead the singing of a gang of workmen was well worth extra pay. This impulse in the Negro to sing at work is inborn; it is a racial trait common to his African forebears. With us Anglo-Saxons, song as a labor invigorator seems to have died away with the invention of machinery, although our parents still remember the "chanty-man" of the merchant sailing vessels whose voice led those lays and ballads which helped to weigh anchor and to hoist, lower or furl the sails. The human instinct which takes the scattered movements of a group at labor and unifies them into a concerted, rhythmic expression, making them one in song, is in itself an art instinct, and in this primitive kind of art the African is a master. Is it not, after all, a most vital and priceless thing, this art which is part of a man's own pulse-beats, his own muscle, his own will? What a contrast to the silent, deadening toil of the modern factory.

We in the United States should be thankful that Hampton Institute has done so much to preserve in living form the old songs of the Negro. Founded in Virginia, in 1868, by General Samuel Chapman Armstrong,[1] Hampton has been the pioneer industrial school for the training of backward races. But though it has taught Negroes and Indians to plow and plant in the white man's way, to support themselves by trades and to meet the economic conditions of the modern world, Hampton has not failed to recognize that the dark-skinned peoples have gifts of their own. More than that, the primitive races —child-races, clasping the mother-hand of Nature—still have a vigorous gladness in life itself and in the proud strength of the human body; while we, already weary in our maturity, feel little but the strain of forced marching on the road to progress, and the fever for the goal. Sophisticated creatures of a complex culture, do we not indeed need the nature-people to call us back to that youth of natural poetry and song wherein work is vitalized by the free play of the imaginative spirit? Believing in the ethnic value of the black men and the red, Hampton has urged her pupils to bring to the school their own folk-lore and music. The saving of this inheritance has been a glorious task, for the dynamic force of the old songs has charged the life of the students with an impetus of true continuity in that the racial Past, with what it held of dignity and worth, beauty and inspiration, has been lovingly gathered up to be carried on into the new day.

[1]See pp. v and 3.

All three of the Cotton-Songs in this collection are sung at Hampton. The first two were discovered by Miss Cora M. Folsom, who since 1880 has practically devoted her life to the school and has been one of its strongest influences for the encouragement of folk-song. But for her awakening touch these quaint and humorous work-songs, already beginning to grow dim in the background of the students' memory, would have died out and been lost. Miss Folsom now has charge of the school-museum which contains a truly unusual collection of African and other curios, and it was in the large exhibition hall, with its balcony over the water, that the colored students gathered around her in the long evenings of a Southern summer to sing these songs for my recording pencil. They danced, they talked, laughed, explained and illustrated, all with an enthusiasm and an unconsciousness that showed the sympathy of their relation to their white-haired friend. On me, these evenings made a never to be forgotten impression—the soft twilight, the stillness over the lawns that sloped to the water's edge, and the voices of these young men of to-day who sang the songs of their fathers' yesterdays against the background of a far distant African past.

COTT'N-PICKIN' SONG

Recorded from the singing of

Ira Godwin	("Lead")	Agriculture
Joseph Barnes	(Tenor)	Tinsmith
William Cooper	(Baritone)	Schoolteacher
Timothy Carper	(Bass)	Bricklayer

This song was brought to Hampton from Florida by a boy named Hill, who had worked on the plantations with the old people among whom the songs of the cottonfield were traditional. His voice was like a reed-pipe, with the old-time break and quaver in it that is so pastoral in suggestiveness, the mere tones calling up the rural South to the memory of one who has seen it, more intimately than could a visual picture. The wide plantations under the hot sun, the tall rows of cotton-plants, the bending Negroes, with here and there a wide-brimmed battered straw hat shading the face of some old man, the black and white contrast of the fluffy cotton bolls and the dark hands and arms —all this one sees with the first bars of the old song whose clear, pentatonic refrain "Cott'n want a-pickin' " carols against its musical background of elemental harmonies like the chirping iteration of a bird-note rising from among the cotton-stalks.

This is indeed a characteristically rustic song, the primitive five-tone scale being clear-cut throughout, even in all the many verses whose delicately marked variants never venture far from the original simple outline, though molded into delightful little rhythmic contrasts by their play around different words.

No one knows how old the song may be, but it would seem to have sprung into life shortly after the Emancipation, for it begins with no less an event than the reading of the proclamation of freedom to the slaves. (And what a picture the simple verse gives in a few words!)

The Negro now labors as a freedman "in er contract," or for a share of the cotton crop. How the black man sometimes fared in this transaction is both humorously and pathetically shown in the verse where "Uncle Billy" comes out of the cotton-sale with no share at all, "Boss" declaring that the Negro in weeding had chopped his own half of the cotton "out wid de grass." Of course, the newly freed ex-slave, without property or education, is in debt— probably to Boss, who perhaps has seen to that and to the payment of those debts "wid cotton," so that Uncle Billy does "well" when, after all his labor in the sun, he has a few cotton seeds to sell, the product of which brings him the "red han'cher you see 'roun' ma neck"! But with characteristic optimism and good will the old Negro tells Boss that he will "try hit once mo'," and the cherry, sweet, monotonous music of his toil is again heard in the cottonfield.

The dialect in these verses from the furthermost South differs slightly from well-known speech-forms common in more Northern States, and adds to the quaintness and picturesqueness of this song of the Florida plantations.

COTT'N-PICKIN' SONG

Dis cott'n want a-pickin'
               so bad,
Dis cott'n want a-pickin'
               so bad,
Dis cott'n want a-pickin'
               so bad,
       Gwine clean all ober dis farm.

One twenties[1] of May mo'nin'
Under dat barnyard tree,
Dem Yankees read dem papers
An' sot dem darkies free.

Dis cott'n want a-pickin'
               so bad,
Dis cott'n want a-pickin'
               so bad,
Dis cott'n want a-pickin'
               so bad,
       Gwine clean all ober dis farm.

I's been workin' in er contract
Eber since dat day,
An' jes' found out dis yur[2]
Why hit[3] didn't pay.

Dis cott'n want a-pickin'
               so bad,
Dis cott'n want a-pickin'
               so bad,
Dis cott'n want a-pickin'
               so bad,
       Gwine clean all ober dis farm.

When Boss sol' dat cott'n
I ask fo' ma half.
He tol' me I chopped out
Ma half wid de grass.

NOTE:—Some singers omit the word "gwine" from the last line of the chorus.
[1] Twentieth. [2] Year. [3] It.

90

Dis cott'n want a-pickin'
              so bad,
Dis cott'n want a-pickin'
              so bad,
Dis cott'n want a-pickin'
              so bad,
       Gwine clean all ober dis farm.

Boss said, "Uncle Billy,
I t'ink you done well
To pay yo' debts wid cott'n,
An' have yo' seeds to sell."

Dis cott'n want a-pickin'
              so bad,
Dis cott'n want a-pickin'
              so bad,
Dis cott'n want a-pickin'
              so bad,
       Gwine clean all ober dis farm.

I sol' dem seeds
Fer five cents er peck,
An' bought dis red han'cher[1]
You see 'roun' ma neck.

Dis cott'n want a-pickin'
              so bad,
Dis cott'n want a-pickin'
              so bad,
Dis cott'n want a-pickin'
              so bad,
       Gwine clean all ober dis farm.

I tol' Boss dis yur
I'd try hit once mo';[2]
He counted off dis cott'n,
Took ev'ry ozzer[3] row.

---

[1] Handkerchief.   [2] More.   [3] Other.

91

Dis cott'n want a-pickin'
                    so bad,
Dis cott'n want a-pickin'
                    so bad,
Dis cott'n want a-pickin'
                    so bad,
          Gwine clean all ober dis farm.

Us plant dis cott'n in Aprul,
Us lay hit by-a in June,
Us had a hot dry summer,
Dat's why hit open so soon.
Dis cott'n want a-pickin'
                    so bad,
Dis cott'n want a-pickin'
                    so bad,
Dis cott'n want a-pickin'
                    so bad,
          Gwine clean all ober dis farm.

Hurry up, chillun,
Us ought ter been gone;
Dis wezzer[1] looks so cloudy
I t'ink hit's gwine ter storm.
Dis cott'n want a-pickin'
                    so bad,
Dis cott'n want a-pickin'
                    so bad,
Dis cott'n want a-pickin'
                    so bad,
          Gwine clean all ober dis farm.

Boy, stop goosin'[2] dat cott'n
An' take better care!
Make-a haste, you lazy rascul,
An' bring dat row from dere!
Dis cott'n want a-pickin'
                    so bad,
Dis cott'n want a-pickin'
                    so bad,
Dis cott'n want a-pickin'
                    so bad,
          Gwine clean all ober dis farm.

[1] Weather.
[2] "Goosing" cotton is to pick so carelessly that some of the cotton is left on the bolls.

92

Cott'n-Pickin' Song

(From Florida)

Recorded
and transcribed by
Natalie Curtis-Burlin

Note. The Hampton Quartet usually sing only the last three verses of this song.

* The voice of the "Lead" or leader carries the melody and is printed in the piano-part in large type. It should sound well above the other voices.

so bad,— Gwine clean all o - ber dis farm.

cott'n want a - pickin' so bad,— Gwine clean all o - ber dis farm. One

so bad,— Gwine clean all o - ber dis farm.

so bad,— Gwine clean all o - ber dis farm.

1st verse
SOLO

twentis * of___ May mo'n - in', Under dat barn - yard tree,— Dem

Yan - kees read___ dem pa - pers,— An' sot dem dark - ies free. Dis

CHORUS *D.S.*

2d verse
SOLO

___ I's been work - in' in er con - tract Eb - er since dat day,— An'

jes' found out___ dis yur ** ___ Why hit *** did - n't pay. Dis

CHORUS *D.S.*

* Twentieth. ** Year. *** It.

3d verse

When Boss sol' dat cot-t'n, I ask fo'— ma half;— He

tol' me— I chopped out— Ma half wid de— grass. Dis

4th verse

Boss said, "Un-cle Bil-ly, I t'ink you done well— To

pay yo'— debts— wid cot-t'n— An' have yo' seeds— to— sell." Dis

5th verse

I so...o.ol' dem see.ee.eeds Fer five cents er peck, An'

bought dis— red han'-cher* You see roun' ma neck. Dis

6th verse

I tol' Boss dis yur— I'd try hit— once mo;** He

counted— off— dis cot-t'n— Took ev'-ry oz-zer*** row. Dis

* Handkerchief. ** More. *** Other.

7th verse

SOLO

Us plant dis cot - t'n in A - prul, Us

lay hit by - a in June,___ Us had a___ hot,___ dry

CHORUS *D. S.*

sum - mer:___ Dat's why hit o - pen so___ soon. Dis

8th verse

SOLO

Hur - ry___ up, chil - lun, Us ought ter___ been gone, ___ Dis

CHORUS *D. S.*

wez - zer* looks___ so cloud-y,___ I t'ink hit's gwine___ ter storm. Dis

9th verse

SOLO

Boy, stop goos - in'** dat cot - t'n,___ An'

take bet - ter care;___ Make - a haste, you la - zy

CHORUS *D. S*

ras - cul,___ An' bring dat row___ from dere! Dis

* Weather.

** "Goosing" cotton, is to pick so carelessly that some of the cotton is left in the bolls.

97

COTT'N-DANCE SONG

Recorded from the singing of

Ira Godwin	("Lead")	Agriculture
Joseph Barnes	(Tenor)	Tinsmith
William Cooper	(Baritone)	Schoolteacher
Timothy Carper	(Bass)	Bricklayer

At Hampton this song is often sung as a companion to the Cott'n-Pickin' Song, following as a spirited climax; for the songs seem to belong together, having been brought from Florida by the same boy[1] of whose life and work in the far South they had formed a part.

The cotton picked, it was hauled to the scales and weighed. Then, to celebrate the end of the labor, the Negroes broke into a jubilant dance, throwing themselves into the sport with the same exuberance and freshness as the tireless native runners and burden carriers of Africa, who at the end of the day dance with a violence that attests to the tremendous physical endurance of the black race. The cotton-pickers, amid shouts and laughter, formed a rough circle with the dancer in the middle. Then a dance-song rose from lusty throats while the encircling singers and onlookers beat a sharp rhythmic accompaniment by stamping their feet, clapping their hands and patting their knees.

Anyone who wanted to dance leaped into the open space in the centre of the circle; then when a dancer tired he fell back and joined the outer ring, where he pounded and clapped and sang with the rest.

This dance-song with its five-tone scale is probably still sung in the Florida cotton-fields, though it reaches back to the days of slavery. It is of course typical of the Negro in America, yet if one has studied African folk-lore and music one may easily trace its remote ancestry to the Dark Continent. For the dance, of which this song is the Europeanized melodic life, is plainly a transplanted and adapted version of the informal social dances of savage Africa, with their rapid intricate pattering dance-step and their rhythmic accompaniment in which the whole human body seems to take syncopated part.

The words are spontaneous echoes of labor in the cottonfields. Any number of verses were made up on the moment to keep the song going as long as the zeal for dancing should last. The whole character of the dance was simply an impulsive overflow of high spirits. Anyone could make up a song, anyone could start in to dance, anyone could prolong the dance by composing a new line or a fresh verse. What charm lies in the infectious gaiety and sweeping rhythm of such an irrepressible outburst in music!

The verses are full of typical local allusions, so condensed as to be mere symbols of the meaning which is perfectly understood by the groups of humanity whose life and thoughts the song reflects—a trait common to

[1] See Cott'n-Pickin' Song, p. 89.

98

much primitive poetry among many races. The song begins with "Massa's"[1] emphatic commands: "O Massa said from firs' to las'." The next lines epitomize the work of the cottonfields, for after the seed is planted in rows about three feet apart, each plant comes up as two little leaves; then the man or woman must take a hoe and weed out all but "two stalks" which must be about "eighteen inches an' a half" apart. Also the weeding must include "all de grass"; Massa is very positive about this. (It will be remembered how in the previous song Boss denies Uncle Billy a share of the cotton picked by saying that the old Negro had "chopped out" his half "wid de grass"—the black man's half being evidently the tiny worthless plants that had to be thrown away anyhow.[2]) On poor land the two little stalks are left nearer together, since the soil will not give them enough nourishment to grow and spread as far as "eighteen inches an' a half"; so that Massa's commands imply good land.[3]

As the song progresses and the random verses are flung out, one seems to see and hear the whole life of the cottonfield—the wail of a baby stung by a cotton-fly; the blinding sun that makes the toiler defend present laziness by the promise to "pick a hundred by an' by"; the race between the cotton-pickers for the wager of a " 'tater-pie," which adds zest and merriment to the labor; finally, the picture of the cotton-pickers themselves in their "duckin' breeches an' baggin' sacks," for every item of their apparel is described. Perhaps, when the cotton is picked and hauled and the labor is over, comes the vision of a gift of new clothes from Massa![4]

"Dem duckin' breeches" are breeches of duck or ducking, usually grayish in color and very strong of wear, sometimes shot with a narrow "pin-stripe." "Baggin' sacks" are the pouches or "sacks" made of bagging and worn at the side to hold the cotton as it is picked. "Red ripper" is a red ribbon—probably a neck-tie; the shoes and hat must "match" only because they must rhyme with "sacks!" Such a song is never a conscious composition—the lines are shouted out as they come into the singers' heads. Meanings really matter little so long as the rhythm and swing and feeling for rhyme are there. There is a child-like charm in the naïveté with which assonance takes the place of rhyme in such words as "last," "half," "grass" and "task," and further on in "sacks," "match" and "back." And, whether intentional or not (perhaps one line was forgotten by the Florida boy or his associates?), the emphasis of the last two lines, identically the same, is most effective in celebrating the climax of the song—the prospect of a feast of " 'possum."

---

[1] Master. [2] See p. 89.

[3] For help in the explanation of this song, I am indebted to the colored students, and to Miss Folsom of Hampton, the original collector of these Negro verses.

[4] See "Peanut-Pickin' Song," Book IV of this series, where Massa rewards his slaves with new clothes.

COTT'N-DANCE SONG

(From Slavery Times)

Florida

O Massa said from firs' to las',
     'Way down—in de cott'n-fiel'
Eighteen inches an' a half,
     'Way down—in de cott'n-fiel'
Two stalks an' all de grass,
     'Way down—in de cott'n-fiel'
So much a day—dat's yo' task,
     'Way down—in de cott'n-fiel'
I t'ought I heard dat baby cry,
     'Way down—in de cott'n-fiel'
Hit may be stung by a cotton-fly
     'Way down—in de cott'n-fiel'
De hotter de sun de redder ma eye,
     'Way down—in de cott'n-fiel'
I'll pick a hundred by an' by.
     'Way down—in de cott'n-fiel'
Jim he bet me a 'tater pie,
     'Way down—in de cott'n-fiel'
Dat he could pick more cott'n dan I.
     'Way down—in de cott'n-fiel'
I straddle dat row an' hit did fly,
     'Way down—in de cott'n-fiel'
I win dat pie an' didn't half try.
     'Way down—in de cott'n-fiel'
I ben' ma head down to dat groun',
     'Way down—in de cott'n-fiel'
Didn't look up till I made dat roun'.
     'Way down—in de cott'n-fiel'
Den dat sun was almos' down,
     'Way down—in de cott'n-fiel'
Jim didn't had but fifty poun'.
     'Way down—in de cott'n-fiel'
Dis cott'n so rank and den so tall,
     'Way down—in de cott'n-fiel'
'T won't be open all by fall.
     Way down—in de cott'n-fiel'
Den we pick hit an' dat'll be all,
     'Way down—in de cott'n-fiel'
Den how we gwine ter get it haul?
     'Way down—in de cott'n-fiel'

Dem duckin' breeches and baggin' sacks,
>'*Way down—in de cott'n-fiel'*
Red ripper, shoes, and hats to match,
>'*Way down—in de cott'n-fiel'*
Big lezzer[1] straps across de back,
>'*Way down—in de cott'n-fiel'*
Dat strongly helt dem baggin' sacks.
>'*Way down—in de cott'n-fiel'*
De possums den in de cott'n pile,
>'*Way down—in de cott'n-fiel'*
De possums den in de cott'n pile,
>'*Way down—in de cott'n-fiel'.*

[1] Leather

Cott'n-Dance Song

Dating from the time of slavery

(From Florida)

* The voice of the "Lead" or leader carries the melody and is printed in the piano-part in large type. It must sound well above the other voices.

* Though the chorus is usually sung _ff_, the dynamics may be altered to give variety.

* "Hit" is "it," in Florida dialect.

hot-ter de sun de red-der ma eye, 'Way down in de cot-t'n-fiel',

(CHORUS)

I'll pick a hun-dred by an' by, 'Way down in de cot-t'n –

(CHORUS)

Jim he bet me a 'ta-ter pie, 'Way down in de cot-t'n-fiel', Dat

(CHORUS)

he could pick more cot-t'n dan I, 'Way down in de cot-t'n – I

(CHORUS)

straddle dat row an' hit did fly, 'Way down in de cot-t'n-fiel', I

(CHORUS)

win dat pie an' did-n't half try, 'Way down in de cot-tn – I

(CHORUS with each repetition)

ben' ma head down to dat groun', 'Way down in de cot-t'n-fiel',

Did-n't look up till I made dat roun', 'Way down in de cot-t'n –

Den dat sun was al-mos' down, 'Way down in de cot-t'n-fiel',

Jim did-n't had but fif-ty poun', 'Way down in de cot-t'n – Dis

cot-t'n so rank an' den so tall, 'Way down in de cot-t'n-fiel',

'Twon't be o-pen all by fall, 'Way down in de cot-t'n–

Den we pick hit an' dat 'll be all, 'Way down in de cot-t'n-fiel. Den

how we gwine ter git hit haul? 'Way down in de cot-t'n– Dem

duck-in' breeches an' bag-gin' sacks, 'Way down in de cot-t'n-fiel,

* ** Red ripper, shoes an hats to match, 'Way down in de cot-t'n–

Big lez-zer straps a-cross de back, 'Way down in de cot-t'n-fiel', Dat

strong-ly helt dem bag-gin' sacks, 'Way down in de cot-t'n– De

pos-sums den in de cot-t'n pile, 'Way down in de cot-t'n-fiel', De

*** pos-sums den in de cot-t'n pile, 'Way down in de cot-t'n-fiel'.

* The song increases in speed towards the end. ** Ribbon.
*** After the chorus, these last words may be repeated spoken, or rather shouted, with slow emphasis. Gay yells follow the ending of the song.

106

COTT'N-PACKIN' SONG

Recorded from the singing of

JAMES E. SCOTT

From Georgia comes this chant of the black laborers at the docks, brought to Hampton by a young Negro, James Scott, now in the United States Army.[1]

In old times the City of Savannah was a great place for the shipping of cotton, and the wharves hummed and rattled as the wheeled hand-trucks, heaped with cotton-bales, were whirled by running Negroes to the side of the vessels. Then a derrick from the ship let down a great hook and hoisted a bale on which knelt a Negro to balance the load. Up went the hook, while cotton and Negro moved slowly through the air; then down through the open hatch into the hold the bale was lowered, to be seized by the waiting packers and stowed away while the hook swung up and out again with the dangling Negro clinging to it. Bale after bale with its human ballast was thus lifted and dropped.

The black packers in the hold, in gangs of from five to ten men, stowed the cotton by means of iron "screws" which squeezed the bales tightly and compactly into the smallest possible space. Each gang was directed by a "header," or head-man, for the labor required precision and skill as well as strength.

To the Negro, to work in unison means to sing; so as the men strained at their task, a laboring chant arose whose fine-toned phrases were regularly cut by a sharp high cry, "*heh!*", which emphasized the powerful twisting of the screws by the rhythmic muscular movement of the singers. Verses without number were made up, and many were the cotton-packing chants of which the one here recorded is a typical example. Though a song of such rudimentary simplicity as this—mere vocalized rhythm—is often intoned in unison without harmony, yet sometimes a singer, musically inclined, would strike in with a tenor or bass part of his own, or add a little embellishing melodic curve to the block-like crudity of the phrases.

Thus the voices of the cotton-packers, embodying as a part of their song the creak of the derrick and the turn of the screw, molded the montonous toil into a form of rhythmic life. And cotton itself, a product of labor under a hot sun and so vital to the economic existence of the Southern States, owes how much to the brawn and blood of the patient Negro—yes, from the planting of the first "eighteen inches an' a half"[2] to the picking of the bolls and the final packing of the bales.

---

[1] James Scott, the singer of this song, is now First Lieutenant in the famous Negro regiment "The Buffaloes" (367th Infantry). At this writing he is reported to have been severely wounded in action.

[2] See Cott'n-Dance Song, p. 100.

COTT'N-PACKIN' SONG

(From Georgia)

Screw dis cott'n,
> *heh!*

Screw dis cott'n,
> *heh!*

Screw dis cott'n,
> *heh!*

> Screw it tight—
>> *heh!*

Screw dis cott'n,
> *heh!*

Screw dis cott'n,
> *heh!*

Screw dis cott'n,
> *heh!*

> Wid all yo' might—
>> *heh!*

Here we come, boys,
> *heh!*

Here we come, boys,
> *heh!*

Here we come, boys,
> *heh!*

> Do it right—
>> *heh!*

Don't get tired,[1]
> *heh!*

Don't get tired,
> *heh!*

Don't get tired,
> *heh!*

> Time ain't long—
>> *heh!*

Keep on workin',
> *heh!*

Keep on workin',
> *heh!*

Keep on workin',
> *heh!*

> Sing dis song—
>> *heh!*

[1] Pronounced in two syllables: *"ti-yerd."*

(These last two verses are modern)
Pay-day here, boys,
                    heh!
Pay-day here, boys,
                    heh!
Pay-day here, boys,
                    heh!
          I hear dem say—
                              heh!

We'll have money,
               heh.
We'll have money,
               heh!
We'll have money
               heh!
          Dis yere day—
                         heh!

Cott'n-Packin' Song

(From Savannah, Georgia)

As brought to Hampton and sung by James Scott

Absolutely rhythmic and rather slow,
with regular and monotonous emphasis ($\mathbf{\downarrow} = 76$)

Voices in Unison

Screw dis cot-t'n! (heh!) Screw dis cot-t'n! (heh!) Screw dis cot-t'n! (heh!)

Screw it tight! (heh!)

Screw dis cot-t'n! (heh!) Screw dis cot-t'n! (heh!) Screw dis cot-t'n! (heh!)

Wid all yo' might! (heh!)

Here we come, boys, (heh!) Here we come, boys, (heh!) Here we come, boys, (heh!)

Do it right! (heh!)

Don't get ti-red, (heh!) Don't get ti-red, (heh!) Don't get ti-red, (heh!)

Time ain't long; (heh!)

Keep on work-in', (heh!) Keep on work-in', (heh!) Keep on work-in', (heh!)

Sing dis song. (heh!)

* This sound is a sharp, rather aspirant ejaculation, accompanying the rhythmic turning of the screw in packing the cotton. It has no pitch.

** Pronounced *"Ti-yerd."* *** "On" pronounced with a long o, *"ōn"* or *"ohn."*

Modern verses, and fresh extempora-neous verses, are added by the Negroes in singing this song ad infinitum.

110

CORN-SHUCKIN' SONG

Recorded from the singing of
Goodwin, Barnes, Cooper, Carper, Lancaster, Scott, and other Hampton boys who gathered
together in an improvised chorus to join in the refrain of this old song.

This vigorous and spirited chant is said to have come originally from Alabama. A description of the old corn-shucking "bees" at which this was sung, is best expressed in the words of the late Booker T. Washington, of whose youth such songs formed a part.

"The simple, natural joy of the Negro in little things converted every change in the dull routine of his life into an event. Hog-killing time was an annual festival, and the corn-shucking was a joyous event which the whites and blacks, in their respective ways, took part in, and enjoyed. These corn-shucking bees, or whatever they may be called, took place during the last of November or the first half of December. They were a sort of prelude to the festivities of the Christmas season. Usually they were held upon one of the larger or wealthier plantations.

"After all the corn had been gathered, thousands of bushels, sometimes, it would be piled up in the shape of a mound, often to the height of fifty or sixty feet. Invitations would be sent around by the master himself to the neighbor-planters, inviting their slaves on a certain night to attend. In response to these invitations, as many as one or two hundred men, women and children would come together.

"When all were assembled around the pile of corn, some one individual, who had already gained a reputation as a leader of singing, would climb on top of the mound and begin at once, in clear loud tones, a solo—a song of the corn-shucking season—a kind of singing which I am sorry to say has very largely passed from memory and practice. After leading off in this way, in clear, distinct tones, the chorus at the base of the mound would join in, some hundred voices strong. The words, which were largely improvized, were very simple and suited to the occasion, and more often than not they had the flavor of camp-meeting rather than any more secular proceeding. Such singing I have never heard on any other occasion."[1]

The pride with which "Massa's niggers" are described as "shining like a beaver hat" makes one think that to the Negro in this country, as to the African on the Dark Continent, a shining skin was a thing of beauty. My Zulu informant[2] told me that the black youths of South Africa often carried a little carved flask (a gourd, or a wooden box) filled with butter from their herds—for Zulus are great herdsmen and their wealth is counted in cattle. Part of the toilet of these youths, superb in the bodily beauty of height, poise and physical development, consisted in rubbing this butter into their skins till their bare black limbs shone like polished ebony. "And then," said the Zulu, "when the sun's rays fell on them, they were beautiful indeed." What a

[1] From "The Story of the Negro." Booker T. Washington; Vol. I, Page 158. (Doubleday, Page & Co., 1909.)

[2] See "African-Songs from the Dark Continent," by Natalie Curtis Burlin. (In press with Doubleday, Page & Co.)

wealth of plastic material these magnificent burnished forms would offer to a modern sculptor! The shining skin suggests, too, the smooth, polished surfaces of African wood-carving, proving how primitive art, tho' so seldom literal in representation, yet *invariably expresses the life of which it is a part.* Thus in songs of work and play—a musical form of decoration and design— the American Negro, like his African ancestor, enriches daily existence with a humble beauty of his own creating.

CORN-SHUCKIN' SONG

Come out hyah an' shuck dis co'n,
Oh! Oh! Oh!
Come out hyah an' shuck dis co'n,
Oh! Oh! Oh!

Bigges' pile seen sence I was bo'n,
Oh! Oh! Oh!
Bigges' pile seen sence I was bo'n,
Oh! Oh! Oh!

Massa's niggers am slick an' fat,
Oh! Oh! Oh!
Shine jes' like a beaver hat,
Oh! Oh! Oh!

Jones's niggers am lean an' po',
Oh! Oh! Oh!
Don' know ef dey git enough to eat o' no,
Oh! Oh! Oh!

In this corn-shucking song as quoted by Booker T. Washington,[1] the first verse is treated as a refrain, repeated throughout the song. This form resembles that of the Spirituals, whose structure consists in what the colored people call "Chorus and Verses."[2]

Refrain
Turn out here and shuck dis corn,
Oh! Oh! Oh!
Biggest pile o' corn seen since I was born,
Oh! Oh! Oh!

[1] "The Story of the Negro," by Booker T. Washington; Vol. I, page 160. (Doubleday, Page & Co., 1909.)
[2] See Forewords to Books I and II of this series.

I.

Massa's niggers am big and fat,
> *Oh! Oh! Oh!*
Shine just like a new beaver hat,
> *Oh! Oh! Oh!*
>> (*Refrain.*)

II.

Jones's niggers am lean and po',
> *Oh! Oh! Oh!*
Don't know whether they get enough to eat or no,
> *Oh! Oh! Oh!*
>> (*Refrain.*)

Corn-Shuckin' Song

(From Virginia)

* The voice of the "Lead," or leader carries the melody and is printed in the piano-part in large type. It must sound well above the other voices.
** Some singers say "Turn out." *** Here.
**** The three ejaculative "Ohs!" throughout this song are sung so legato that they are blended into one long sound, almost as tho' the singers sang "Oh - wo - wo!"

* Ossia:

** Here the bass really sings *"Oh - wo-ho - wo!"*

Another version of the song gives a somewhat different rhythmic value of the notes of the refrain, as follows:

BOOK IV

WORK- and PLAY-SONGS

Foreword and introductory notes   123

Peanut-Pickin' Song

Notes   129   /   Music   131

Hammerin' Song

Notes   140   /   Music   146

Lullaby

Notes   149   /   Music   150

"Chicka-Hanka"

Notes   153   /   Music   154

"Hyah, Rattler!"

Notes   155   /   Music   157

"Old Rags, Bottles, Rags!"

Notes   156   /   Music   157

'Liza-Jane

Notes   158   /   Music   160

FOREWORD

IN the South, a white musician stumbles upon experiences that may be counted as among the most awakening of his life, for there the spirit of the Negro is often loosed in music that makes one wonder at the possibilities of the race. Far down in Alabama where the "Black Belt" is broad and the Negroes outnumber the whites, I touched upon something that class-rooms and concert-halls rarely hold,—nothing less than the primitive essence of untaught and unteachable creative art.

It was at the Calhoun Industrial School[1] (whose existence was inspired by the example of Hampton Institute) that a great meeting of colored people was held one year to listen to discussions by Northern white scholars concerning the advancement of their race. Over tawny roads that stretched beneath tall pine trees came the people of the "Black Belt" in wagons and astride of plodding mules; brown mules, black mules, lemon-colored mules—they came with their dusky riders from all directions in an endless stream, and I particularly remember the flash of a red petticoat across a white mule glinting through the green. Such shining good-natured faces,—pure Negroes these with little admixture of white blood, representing different types of the many tribes brought from all parts of Africa by the slave-trade, through which captives from the far interior and from the opposite coasts of the Dark Continent were finally landed in America. Some of the men were tall, and their aquiline noses and pointed beards told of the strain of Arab and other Semitic blood that runs through many a native of Africa's East Coast; others were swart and thick-set, with flat noses and heavy lips. Many were so ebony black that the shadows in their smooth skins seemed a soft gray-purple, like deep ripe grapes. No European peasantry could have offered to the painter more striking material than these dark-skinned sinewy people in their blue jeans and bright calicoes amid the deep tones of the pines.

They hitched their animals in the woods and gathered in a cleared space under the trees. These colored folk had come many miles over mountain and valley from their crude log-cabins, and they assembled long before the hour. To them this gathering had almost the significance of a religious service, a "Camp-meet'n" of the olden time. Seated in rows, reverent and silent, they waited for something to happen. And as they sat, patient in the early warmth of the April sun, suddenly a rhythmic tremor seemed to sway over the group as a sweep of wind stirs grasses; there arose a vibration, an almost inaudible hum—was it from the pine trees or from this mass of humanity?— and then the sound seemed to mold itself into form, rhythmic and melodic, taking shape in the air, and out from this floating embryo of music came the refrain of a song quavered by one voice, instantly caught up by another— till soon the entire gathering was rocking in time to one of the old plantation melodies! Men, women and children sang, and the whole group swung to and

---

[1] A remarkable collection of Negro Spirituals has been made for the Calhoun School by Miss Emily Halowell: "*Calhoun Plantation Songs.*"

fro and from side to side with the rhythm of the song, while many of the older people snapped their fingers in emphasis like the sharp click of an African gourd rattle.

It was spirited singing and it was devout; but the inspirational quality of the group-feeling made this music seem a lambent, living thing, a bit of "divine fire" that descended upon these black people like the gift of tongues. It was as though the song had first hovered in the trees above their swaying forms, intangible, till one of them had reached up and seized it, and then it had spread like flame. And as usual with Negroes, this was extemporaneous part-singing,—women making up alto, men improvising tenor or bass, the music as a whole possessed so completely by them all (or so utterly possessing them!) that they were free to abandon themselves to the inspiration of their own creative instinct.

Often in the South I heard this same strange breathless effect of a song being born among a group simultaneously, descending, as it were, from the air. On a suffocatingly hot July Sunday in Virginia, in a little ramshackle meeting-house that we had approached over a blinding road nearly a foot deep in dust, a number of rural Negroes had gathered from an outlying farm, dressed all in their dust-stained Sunday best for the never-to-be-omitted Sabbath service. Their intense and genuine piety with its almost barbaric wealth of emotion could not but touch a visitor from the cold North. The poverty of the little. church was in itself a mute appeal for sympathy. A gaudy and somewhat ragged red table cloth covered the crude pulpit on which rested a huge and very battered Bible,—it had probably sustained many vigorous thumps during the high-flown exhortations of the gilt-spectacled preacher. A crazy lamp, tilted side-ways, hung from the middle of the ceiling. Through the broken window-shutters (powerless to keep out the diamond glare of the morning sun) came slits of light that slanted in syncopated angles over the swarthy people, motes dancing in the beams. No breeze; the sticky heat was motionless; from afar came a faint sound of chickens clucking in the dust. Service had already begun before we came and the congregation, silent and devout, sat in rows on rough backless benches. The preacher now exhorted his flock to prayer and the people with one movement surged forward from the benches and down onto their knees, every black head deep-bowed in an abandonment of devotion. Then the preacher began in a quavering voice a long supplication. Here and there came an uncontrolable cough from some kneeling penitent or the sudden squall of a restless child; and now and again an ejaculation, warm with entreaty, "O Lord!" or a muttered "Amen, Amen"—all against the background of the praying, endless praying.

Minutes passed, long minutes of strange intensity. The mutterings, the ejaculations, grew louder, more dramatic, till suddenly I felt the creative thrill dart through the people like an electric vibration, that same half-audible hum arose,—emotion was gathering atmospherically as clouds gather—and then, up from the depths of some "sinner's" remorse and imploring came a pitiful little plea, a real Negro "moan," sobbed in musical cadence. From somewhere in that bowed gathering another voice improvised a response: the plea sounded again, louder this time and more impassioned; then other voices joined in the answer, shaping it into a musical phrase; and so, before our ears, as one might say, from this molten metal of music a new song was smithied out, composed then and there by no one in particular and by everyone in general.

With the Negro, it would seem that the further back one traces the current of musical inspiration that runs through the race, (that is, the more primitive the people and thus the more instinctive the gift), the nearer does one come to the divine source of song,—intuition, which is in turn the well-spring of all genius. So often does education deaden and even utterly destroy intuitive art in individuals as in races, that one might affirm that the genius is he who can survive the attrition of scholastic training! Certainly no sophisticated part-singing sounds in my memory with the poignant charm of the unconscious music which I heard one day in a big tobacco factory in the South where a group of utterly illiterate and ignorant black laborers were sorting tobacco leaves in a dusty, barren room. Rough sons and daughters of toil, ragged and unkempt, no one could accuse them of ever having come under the smooth influence of "refined white environment." Crude and primitive they were in looks as in speech. Yet I never heard collective voices that were sweeter or that appealed more immeasurably to the imagination with their penetrating, reedlike beauty of quality. The fields, the hot sun, the open sky sang through them. And the harmonies with which these workers adorned their half barbaric melodies seemed prismatic in their brilliant unmodulated grouping of diatonic chords, their sudden interlocking of unrelated majors and minors, and their unconscious defiance of all man-made laws of "voice progressions." Such rich, colorful music, (and in my memory I cannot separate the sound of it from the picture of the tobacco leaves in the brown hands), it seemed as though these singers painted with their voices that barren room. And I thought "Yes,—that is the Negro. So he has done always. With song he has colored his shadowed life, evoking hope, joy, beauty even, from within himself."

Yet in the voices of these toilers lingered an indescribable pathos, a something both child-like and touching. For with all his brawn, his good-humor, and his wide, ready smile, the Negro, when he sings, tells something of that shadow that only song can lighten. Probably no blacks in the country were more backward than these factory-hands, laboring so monotonously in the lazy haze of Southern heat,—a heat that puts one's brain to sleep. That they could sing extemporaneously in harmonies that not only approached real art but that touched one's very soul, seemed a proof that though this is still a child-race, the long path of human evolution and advance stretches before it in endless promise. Is it not in the Song of the Negro that we glimpse the spirit of the race reaching forward toward development and eventual unfolding? And when we see that song illumining with an inner light multitudes otherwise darkly inarticulate and groping, we think of Emerson and ponder: The Negro 'Over-Soul'—is it Music?

NATALIE CURTIS-BURLIN.

THE untaught instinct of the Negro to turn life into music is given full freedom to expand and develop at Hampton Institute, Virginia, the school for Negroes and Indians on which have been patterned Tuskegee Institute and the Calhoun School in Alabama; the Penn School at St. Helena Island, South Carolina; and other industrial training schools for backward races all over the world, as well as the great system of Government Schools for Indians in the United States.[1]

Among those devoted co-workers whom General Armstrong,[2] founder of Hampton, drew about him in the early days of the school—those days of struggle when the Hampton idea of the correlation of "hand, head and heart" in education was a new and radical experiment—among those who gave their whole lives for the furtherance of Armstrong's purpose and to the fulfillment of his prophecy was Cora M. Folsom,[3] whom the Indian students called "Mother" and whom the Negroes knew as a friend of unfailing sympathy and understanding. It was she who kept alive at Hampton the old Work- and Play-Songs recorded in this volume and in Book III of this series, and it was with her help that I was able to gather up these songs and set them upon paper for the coming generations.

The "Peanut-Pickin' Song" and the "Hammerin' Song" were sung for me by Ira Goodwin, Joseph Barnes, William Cooper and Timothy Carper, all Hampton students; but in the singing of the "Lullaby" and "'Liza-Jane" the quartet was augmented by James E. Scott, Page Lancaster, Benjamin Davis and other young men who "dropped in" during recreation hours at the school to add their voices and their sunny laughter to this work of record. Most of these "boys" who sang so gaily and light-heartedly and danced as they sang, answered their country's call and went singing into the service of the United States Army. Some are now safely returned from Europe, some have been wounded and some will never sing again. But those who went "West" have, like their fellows, left the echo of their voices in France. The old songs that upheld the soul of the Negro race during the long years of bondage in America, were carried into the greatest concerted human struggle that mankind has ever known. Said a French General, "It was not alone the colored troops that were helped by the songs of the Negroes, but the white people as well. Far and near, the black soldiers cheered with their singing all who came within sound of their voices; officer and private, villager and peasant alike—none will ever forget the stirring effect of those old Negro songs." In the history of the war, memory will sound a pleasanter note for the singing of the Negro over-seas.

1See Foreword, Book I.
2See p. 3.
3See p. 88.

THESE RECORDS OF

NEGRO WORK- AND PLAY-SONGS

ARE DEDICATED TO

HENRY T. BURLEIGH

NEGRO music in America has had as one of its prophets and standard-bearers a colored artist of great dignity, simplicity and worth: Henry T. Burleigh, singer and composer.

It was very early in life that the racial love of music found insistent expression in "Harry Burleigh," as he is affectionately called by whites and blacks. For as a child he paid with pneumonia for the joy of hearing a great pianist play. Kneedeep in snow but oblivious to the cold he had stood for hours outside the window of a house in Erie where Rafael Joseffy was giving a recital. His illness and the cause of it attracted the interest of the lady (Mrs. E. C. Russell) in whose house Joseffy had played, and she subsequently arranged that "Harry" should open the door for guests whenever she had music at her home, so that in this way he could listen without danger. So Burleigh was privileged to hear many of the great artists of the day, and this contact led to his receiving a scholarship at the National Conservatory of Music in New York, where he advanced so rapidly that he soon became assistant instructor in several branches of study. It was here that the friendship between the young colored man and Anton Dvořák was formed, for the Bohemian composer had accepted at that time the post of musical director of the Conservatory. And it was Burleigh's singing of the old Negro melodies which in a great measure gave to Dvořák that contact with Negro folk-music which formed the background for the themes of his own creating in the "Symphony from the New World."

Nor did Burleigh's association with the best in art ever lead him away from the music of his race. On the contrary, it is he, the foremost singer whom the race so far has produced, who has steadily upheld the value and beauty of true Negro music. On his concert programs, along with the songs of great composers, he has always placed a group of the old Negro Spirituals, thus telling the world that this racial music of his people is worthy to be heard beside the great songs of Art. Nor has he ever shared that instinctive turning away from the old melodies that has characterized many modern colored people. For to him the Spirituals were not to be looked down on and wilfully ignored as reminders of a condition of servitude, but rather to be revered as living proof of a race's spiritual ascendency over-oppression and humiliation.

Never has Henry Burleigh sunk the high standard of his art or commercialized the sacred heritage of his people's song. Quietly, unassumingly, but with singular strength of purpose and conviction he has fought for and won a foremost place among the great artists of America, taking with him the

127

Negro folk-song. As singer he is known on the concert platforms of our finest musical organizations, and as composer of songs and choruses his name is found on programs throughout the country. For over a quarter of a century he has been solo baritone of the white choir at St. George's Church, New York, and for many years he has also sung in the choir of the Jewish Temple Emanu-El.

The Negro race in America looks to Henry Burleigh with no greater respect than does the white race which acclaims him as one of the modest builders of a truly American art. To him, and to all that he has stood for, the recording of these songs is dedicated. Nor may we omit full recognition of those other professional Negro musicians who are now also striving worthily to emphasize the Negro's contribution to the art of this land: R. Nathaniel Dett, J. Rosamond Johnson, Will Marion Cook, Carl Diton, Mrs. E. Azalia Hackley, the Work brothers of Fiske University, and other colored composers and performers in different parts of the country. For the fact that better days are now dawning for Negro artists in America is due in no small degree to the example of Burleigh, and to the perserverance and devotion of all these pioneers who through sacrifice and struggle are trying to lift the standard of the Negro musician and to help dissolve the "color-line" through Art.

PEANUT-PICKIN' SONG

THIS song dates from the days of slavery, when it was sung on the peanut-plantations of a Virginian "Massa." Its quaint verses offer a glimpse of the Southland of the olden days. It is autumn, and in the open air a bonfire sends its welcome glow to the warmth-loving Negroes clustered around it, sitting on the ground, busily picking the harvested peanuts from their stems. Old women with bandanna turbans, old men in wide, battered hats, boys and girls, slaves of all ages are singing the peanut-picking song as the "peas" slip through their brown fingers into the waiting baskets. The gathering has something of that social coming-together in labor noted by Booker T. Washington in his description of the corn-shucking "bees" of slave-times.[1] To make work social, joyous, songful, is the natural instinct of primitive people: this it is that gives life to labor which in modern times too often yields death to the soul of the worker. The Negro on the great plantations knew how to enrich the lot of the slave: with song he kept his spirit from "sinkin' down."[2]

In this old chant the "Big House," the white-columned colonial mansion of the slaveholder, seems to stretch forth a kindly and affectionate hand to the simple black man, rewarding him for his long toil by a personal gift. "Chris'-mus shoes" and the "ol' coat" are evidently instances of "Massa's" approval of the full basket and sack, for all the peanuts seem indeed to have been "picked off" by the faithful laborers whose singing voices made part of the industrial life of the South.

The "walkin'-cane" with which the slave expects to "strut down de Big House lane" is perhaps as bold an imaginative flight as golden slippers in Heaven—for the cane was peculiarly the property of the white *"gentleman,"* and only the freed Negro was allowed to carry it. Hence, perhaps, the great popularity of the slender little walking-stick among the colored race.

This "Peanut-Pickin' Song" was brought to Hampton by a Negro boy named Weldon George, who came from Suffolk County, Virginia, where quantities of peanuts are grown, and where the old song is still heard. The melody has a lightsome, lilting rhythm, almost like that of a dance, and its rural character is emphasized by the five-tone scale. The verses show the care-free, unselfconscious, half-humorous spontaneity of the true folk-poem. Particularly delightful is the last verse, where "Dat ol' 'possum up de tree" is of course waiting to be caught and to end the labor among the peanut-vines with the best reward of all—"dumplin' pies!"

PEANUT-PICKIN' SONG

You kin do jes'-a[3] what you please,
I's gwine ter pick off-a Massa's peas,
I's gwine ter pick off-a Massa's peas,
      An' den I's gwine home.

---

[1]See "Co'n-Shuckin' Song." Book III, this Series.
[2]Some of the old songs bear the refrain "Keep me from sinkin' down."
[3]Just.

I kin fill dis baskit if I choose,
    Den I's gwine home—
Den Massa gwine give me Chris'mus shoes,
    Den I's gwine home—
Two red han'k'chiefs an' a walkin'-cane,
    Den I's gwine home—
Den I's gwine strut down de Big House lane,
    Den I's gwine home.

      Oh,
You kin do jes'-a what you please,
I's gwine ter pick off-a Massa's peas,
I's gwine ter pick off-a Massa's peas,
    An' den I's gwine home.

Fill dis baskit an' dis ol' sack,
    Den I's gwine home—
Den ol' Massa, when he gits back,
    Den I's gwine home—
Gwine ter sen' me to de Big House fer ter git off dat rack,
    Den I's gwine home—
His ol' coat fer ter put on[1] ma back,
    Den I's gwine home.

      Oh,
You kin do jes'-a what you please,
I's gwine ter pick off-a Massa's peas,
I's gwine ter pick off-a Massa's peas,
    An' den I's gwine home.

Dat ol' possum is up de tree,
    Den I's gwine home—
I bet he's waitin' dere fer me,
    Den I's gwine home—
I's gwine ketch him 'less he flies,
    Den I's gwine home—
Den talk 'bout dem dumplin' pies!
    Den I's gwine home.

      Oh,
You kin do jes'-a what you please,
I's gwine ter pick off-a Massa's peas,
I's gwine ter pick off-a Massa's peas,
    An' den I's gwine home.

---

[1]Pronounced in Negro dialect with a long o, *ohn.*

Peanut-Pickin' Song

From Suffolk County, Virginia.

* The voice of the "Lead" (Leader) carries the melody and is printed in the piano-part in large type. It must sound above the other voices.

** can. *** just.

Mas - sa's peas,— An' den I's gwine home. Oh!

Mas - sa's peas,— An' den I's gwine home. Oh!

Mas - sa's peas,— An' den I's gwine home. Oh!

Mas - sa's peas,— An' den I's gwine home. Oh!

You kin do jes'- a what you please,— I's gwine ter pick off - a

You kin do jes'- a what you please,— I's gwine ter pick off - a

You kin do jes' what you please,— I's gwine pick off

You kin do jes'- a what you please,— I's gwine ter pick off

Mas - sa's peas,_____ I's gwine ter pick off - a

Mas - sa's peas,_____ I's gwine ter pick off - a

Mas - sa's peas,_____ I's gwine pick off

Mas - sa's peas,_____ I's gwine ter pick off - a

Fine

Mas - sa's peas,___ An' den I's gwine home.___

Mas - sa's peas,___ An' den I's gwine home.___

Mas - sa's peas,___ An' den I's gwine home.___

Mas - sa's peas,___ An' den I's gwine home.___

Fine

Den I's gwine home.___

Two red han-k-chiefs an' a walk-in'- cane,___ Den I's gwine home.___

Den I's gwine home.___

Den I's gwine home.___

Chorus *D.C.*

Den I's gwine home. Oh!

Den I's gwine strut down de Big House lane,___ Den I's gwine home. Oh!

Den I's gwine home. Oh!

Den I's gwine home. Oh!

Den I's gwine home,——

sen'me to de Big House fer ter git off——dat rack, Den I's gwine home,——

Den I's gwine home,——

Den I's gwine home,——

Chorus *D.C.*

Den I's gwine home. Oh!

His ol' coat—— fer ter put on ma back,—— Den I's gwine home. Oh!

Den I's gwine home. Oh!

Den I's gwine home. Oh!

* "O" is pronounced long in Negro dialect: "ohn".

Chorus *D.C.*

Den I's gwine home,____

I's gwine ketch him 'less he flies, Den I's gwine home,____

Den I's gwine home,____

Den I's gwine home,____

Den I's gwine home. Oh!

Den talk 'bout dem dumplin' pies!____ Den I's gwine home. Oh!

Den I's gwine home. Oh!

Den I's gwine home. Oh!

* catch

139

HAMMERIN' SONG

IN the mines of Virginia this "Hammerin' Song" chimed with the ringing of the hammer as the men chanted the simple pentatonic refrain which gave rhythm and pace to monotonous toil. The improvised verses were usually started by the "header" or headman, who received extra pay for his good voice, his quick musical fancy and his ability to keep the men singing and thus working in unison. "An' as soon we'd git started a-*singin'*," a Negro explained, "we'd forgit we was ti-yerd, an' so long as the header would keep de song a-goin', we'd keep ohn a-hammerin' an' *a-hammerin'!*"

Any number of verses may be sung to this chant, whose sole purpose is the rhythmizing of labor. Usually it is the header who sings alone, for the worker must keep his lungs full while swinging the heavy hammer. Yet sometimes the men break into harmony, joining in after the first notes, when they catch the words. The song is created and re-created by the instinctive play of musical imagination around the rhythm of the hammer's steady stroke. For the unerring artistic sense of these crude singers prompts them to make the very sound of the blow itself (accompanied by the sharp *"huh"* of their own breath) a part of the song, and it is just this extraordinary fusion of the rhythm of men's toiling bodies with the beat of music that makes the work-chants of the Negro typical racial expressions.

This song was brought to Hampton by a boy named George Alston, who had sung it in the mines. The life and death of the miner as well as his surroundings and even his thoughts are hammered out in this vivid and primitive chant. First we hear the summons of the header:

> Boss is callin'
> Let her drive, boys,
> > Foller me,
> > Foller me!

Next the boast,

> Ain't no hammer
> In dis mountain
> > Ring like mine,
> > Ring like mine!

And then the challenge,

> Hammerin' man, you
> Can't beat me,
> > I'll go down,
> > I'll go down.

And again:

> Ef I beat you
> To de bottom,
> > Don't git mad,
> > Don't git mad!

There must surely be an incentive to competition in the verse

> Ef I leads yer,
> O my partner,
> > Don't git mad,
> > Don't git mad!

140

And perhaps there is a note of good-natured irony (or is it good-natured pity and care for a weaker brother) in the words,

> Hammerin' man, don't
> Hammer so hard,
>   You'll break down,
>   You'll break down!

The dream of the miner as to the spending of his hard-won wage, "all in gold" and alas, so quickly gone; his impression of the events of the mine; and the thoughts of home, of "my poor mommer," and of "wife an' chillun," all are very human and are the more poignant in expression because so simply uttered. Nor may we forget the strain of the labor and the miner's constant realization of danger,

> Dese ol' rocks in
> Dis yere mountain
>   Hu'ts my side,
>   Hu'ts my side.
> Ain't no use ter
> Sen' fer de docter,
>   Water-boy's dade,
>   Water-boy's dade!

And again:

> Ef you miss dis
> Two-foot jumper,
>   You'll kill me dade,
>   You'll kill me dade!

How the boy who carried the water met his end in the mines is not explained. But it was indeed a "nine-poun' hammer" that killed "John Henry," who was evidently one of the best workmen, and whose death must have made a deep impression. Nevertheless, the singer boasts that the "nine-poun' hammer" can't kill *him*; he is "gwine home to his wife an' chillun," taking with him a "cake fer baby."

It is a crude, disjointed song, hewn out in the rough by the hammer itself; but it is a bit of reality—of beating, pulsing life, and it glints with a touch of poetry when the miner, up from the bowels of the earth, feels the breath of the heavens in his face, and asks, whether in fiction or in truth,

> Did yo' ever
> Stan' on mountain,
>   In er cloud,
>   In er cloud?
> Did yo' ever
> Wash yo' han's
>   In er cloud,
>   In er cloud?

What a picture the song invokes with its play of man's muscles and of man's daring against the rocks of the mountain, towering cloudward. Men, black men, climbing down and down into the heart of the mountain; ringing hammers making the rocks cry out in echoing pain; deep shadows, deep mysteries, sudden violent death; the spotting flare of little lights; the cross-sections of beams, the swinging bodies,—and then, through the clank and pound of iron on stone, the sound of men's voices rising strong, rough, but tuneful, carving melody out of toil and blackness, mining and bringing to the light the rich ore of art which to the creative spirit lies hidden in even the dull facts and the routine of daily existence.

To have lost art out of the life of the worker is one of the most deadening blights of commercial civilization. Wherever still possible, humanity should hold fast to its God-given power of weaving some beauty of its own fashioning, some thread of personal interest through self-expression, into the woof of labor. For work, all work, is one of the great rhythms of life, and this the Negro exemplifies in his song. See how individual is the Negro's rhythmic invention in even such a simple chant as this one, built around a pounding hammer; and note how typical of the black man's sense of syncopation is the scanning of verses shown in the line-division and accentuation of the shouted phrases.

The folk-poems of these work-songs, mirroring as they do the daily life of black laborers, are gems in the literature of the United States, valuable both for their intrinsic interest—historically, poetically, socially—and for their worth as "human documents." They are alive; and the spirit of song that gave them birth should continue to live, not alone in the Negro's contribution to American letters, but in all the work of the race, from the humblest to the highest.

HAMMERIN' SONG

Boss is call-in'—huh!*
Let her drive, boys—huh!*
        Foller me—huh!*
        Foller me—huh!*

I been hammer-in'—huh!
In dis moun-tain—huh!
        Four long year—huh!
        Four long year—huh!

Ain't no ham-mer—huh!
In dis moun-tain—huh!
        Ring like mine—huh!
        Ring like mine—huh!

Capt'n tol'-me—huh!
Heard ma ham-mer—huh!
        Forty-nine mile—huh!
        Forty-nine mile—huh!

*Hammer falls here, while the men expel their breath with a sharp ejaculation.

Everybo-dy—huh!
What talks 'bout hammer-in'—huh!
        Don't know how—huh!
        Don't know how—huh!

Hammerin' man, you—huh!
Can't beat me—huh!
        I'll go down—huh!
        I'll go down—huh!

Ef I beat you—huh!
To de bot-tom—huh!
        Don't git mad—huh!
        Don't git mad—huh!

Ef I leads yer—huh!
O my part-ner—huh!
        Don't git mad—huh!
        Don't git mad—huh!

Hammerin' man, don't—huh!
Hammer so hard—huh!
        You'll break down—huh!
        You'll break down—huh!

Dis ol' ham-mer—huh!
Keep on ring-'in—huh!
        Roun' ma hade[1]—huh!
        Roun' ma hade—huh!

Dese ol' rocks in—huh!
Dis yere moun-tain—huh!
        Hu'ts[2] my side—huh!
        Hu'ts my side—huh!

Ain't no use ter—huh!
Sen' fer de doc-ter—huh!
        Water-boy's dade[3]—huh!
        Water-boy's dade—huh!

[1]Head.
[2]Hurts.
[3]Dead.

Did yo' ev-er—huh!
Stan' on moun-tain—huh!
    In er cloud—huh!
    In er cloud—huh!

Did yo' ev-er—huh!
Wash yo' han's—huh!
    In er cloud—huh!
    In er cloud—huh!

If you miss dis—huh!
Two-foot jump-er—huh!
    You'll kill me dade—huh!
    You'll kill me dade—huh!

I was hammer-in'—huh!
Las' Decem-ber—huh!
    Wind blow cold—huh!
    Wind blow cold—huh!

I had then 'bout—huh!
Forty-nine dol-lars—huh!
    All in gold—huh!
    All in gold—huh!

Thought I buy me—huh!
Horse an' bug-gy—huh!
    An' ride er-roun'—huh!
    An' ride er-roun'—huh!

If I had jes'—huh!
Forty-nine dol-lars—huh!
    I'd be gone—huh!
    I'd be gone—huh!

Capt'n, when you—huh!
Comin' o-ver—huh!
    Nex' pay-day—huh!
    Nex' pay-day—huh!

Mom' an' Pop-per—huh!
Keeps on writ-in'—huh!
    Thinks I'm dade—huh!
    Thinks I'm dade—huh!

Tryin' t' get liv-in'—huh!
My poor Mom-mer—huh!
               'Tis so hard—huh!
               'Tis so hard—huh!

Ef I could ham-mer—huh!
Like John Hen-ry—huh!
               I'll be gone—huh!
               I'll be gone—huh!

Take my ham-mer—huh!
Give to Cap-t'n—huh!
               Say I'm gone—huh!
               Say I'm gone—huh!

Nine-poun' ham-mer—huh!
Kill John Hen-ry—huh!
               Can't kill me—huh!
               Can't kill me—huh!

I's gwine see my—huh!
Wife an' chil-lun—huh!
               I's gwine home—huh!
               I's gwine home—huh!

Gwine ter git a—huh!
Cake fer ba-by—huh!
               I's gwine home—huh!
               I's gwine home—huh!

Hammerin' Song

From the mines of Virginia

This song is sometimes sung with the "Header" chanting each verse first as a solo, and the gang of men repeating it afterwards in choral harmonies; see p. 148.

As a rule, however, hard labor such as hammering takes all the breath of the men, so that the song is most often sung alone by the "Header."

Slowly and steadily, with heavy, rhythmic beat

Boss is call-in,' *(huh!)* Let her drive, boys, *(huh!)* Fol-ler me,___ *(huh!)* Fol-ler me! *(huh!)* Boss is me!

(huh!) I been ham-mer-in,' *(huh!)* In dis moun-tain, *(huh!)* Four long year,___ *(huh!)* Four long year.

* The "Header" is the head-man in a gang of workers who leads the singing and often receives extra pay for his ability to keep the men working steadily by rhythmizing labor with song. See foreword to Book III, this series, and p. 140.

** The two beats of the measure are so heavily accented that the sixteenth-note has no value in itself and could be written as a grace-note.

*** Hammer falls here. The note indicated is for time-value only; it has no pitch. The "*huh*" is a sharp sound caused by the sudden expelling of the breath as the men throw all their force into the blow.

huh!) Ain't no ham-mer *(huh!)* In dis mountain *(huh!)* Ring like

mine,— *(huh!)* Ring like mine.

(huh!) Cap-t'n tol' me *(huh!)* Heard ma ham-mer *(huh!)* For-ty-nine

mile,— *(huh!)* For-ty-nine mile.

(huh!) Ev-'ry - bo - dy *(huh!)* What talks 'bout ham-mer-in' *(huh!)* Don't know

how,— *(huh!)* Don't know how.

(huh!) Ham-merin' man, you *(huh!)* Can't beat me, *(huh!)* I'll go

down,— *(huh!)* I'll go down. *etc.*

Hammerin' Song

Choral Harmonies

* Sixteenth-notes like grace-notes.
** Basses who cannot take the low *C* may go up.

LULLABY

THIS little lullaby is sung with a crooning softness. It is the song with which the devoted slave-nurse lulled to sleep the children of her master. Though the lullaby is indeed "Mammy's" own song, the colored boys at Hampton delight to sing it, and the mellow sweetness of their voices softens the incongruity of a lullaby sung by men. In fact, as they sing, I dream again of my old Negro "Uncle," my grandmother's cook, who used to carry me high on his shoulder. My childhood held no gentler luxury than when tired out with play, I was sung to sleep by the tender, wistful voice of "Uncle Hen'y."

The pentatonic *Variant* of this lullaby was given me by Mrs. Paul Phipps (Nora Langhorne, of Virginia), who heard it from her Negro "Mammy."

The following quotation[1] from Booker T. Washington describes the affectionate relation between the Negro slave and the children of the master.

"The Negro in exile neither pined away nor grew bitter. On the contrary, as soon as he was able to adjust himself to the conditions of his new life, his naturally cheerful and affectionate disposition began to assert itself. Gradually the natural human sympathies of the African began to take root in the soil of the New World and, growing up spontaneously, twine about the life of the white man by whose side the black man now found himself. The slave soon learned to love the children of his master and they loved him in return."

LULLABY

Go ter sleep,
Go ter sleep,
Go ter sleepy, Mammy's baby.
When you wake
You shall have cake;
Go ter sleepy, Mammy's baby.

Go ter sleep,
Go ter sleep,
Go ter sleepy, Mammy's baby.
All dem horsis
In de stable
B'longs ter Mammy's lit'l baby.

VARIANT

Go ter sleep
Baby-chil',[2]
Go ter sleepy, Mammy's baby.
When you wake
You will have
All de pritty lit'l horsis.

Black an' blue
An' sorrel, too,
All de pritty lit'l horsis.
Hush-a-bye,
Don't you cry,
Go ter sleep, ma lit'l baby-bye!

[1]From "The Story of the Negro." Booker T. Washington (Doubleday, Page & Co., N. Y., 1909).
[2]Child.

149

Lullaby

* The voice of the "Lead" or leader carries the melody and is written in the piano part in large type. It should sound above the other voices.

When you wake You shall have cake,———
All de hors - is in de sta - ble

When you wake You shall have cake,———
All de hors - is in de sta - ble

When you shall have cake,
All de hors - is in de sta - ble

When you wake You shall have cake,
All de hors - is in de sta - ble

Go ter sleep - y, Mam - my's ba - - by.
B'longs ter Mam - my's lit - tle ba - - by.

Go ter sleep - y Mam - my's ba - - by.
B'longs ter Mam - my's lit - tle ba - - by.

Go ter sleep - y Mam - my's ba - - by.
B'longs ter Mam - my's lit - tle ba - - by.

Go ter sleep - y Mam - my's ba - - by.
B'longs ter Mam - my's lit - tle ba - - by.

Sung through a third time humming. Or, the song may be sung throughout as a *Solo* by the voice of the "Lead", with the other voices merely humming the harmonies.

151

Variant

Go ter sleep, ba - by chil', Go ter sleep, ma lit-'l' ba - by.

Hush - a - bye, Don't you cry, Go ter sleep, ma lit-'l' ba - by.

When you wake you will have All de pret-ty lit-'l' hors - is.

Black an'—blue, sor - rel too, All de pret-ty lit-'l' hors - is.

Black an' blue an' sor - rel too, All de pret-ty lit-'l' hors - is.

Hush - a - bye, Don't you cry, Go ter sleep, ma lit-'l' ba -by, bye.

* Pronounced almost like "*li-'l'.*"

** Portamento with each of these phrases.

"CHICKA-HANKA"

HERE is an instance of how a simple order to black men working on the railroad is artistically (one may well use the word) improvised upon until a rhythmic little work-song grows up of itself, and music accompanies the puffing of the locomotives and the slow turning of the wheels of the "side-tracked" train. And with what keen musical perception of sound and rhythm is this steaming and puffing and wheeling of a train expressed in the humorous syllables, "chicka-hanka, chicka-hanka, chicka-hanka!"

It was Mrs. Paul Phipps (Nora Langhorne) who heard this song in Virginia, and from whose singing I made my first notes. The colored boys at Hampton soon made the song their own and sang it in chorus.

> Cap'n, go side-track yo' train!
> > (*Chicka-hanka, chicka-hanka, chicka-hanka!*)
> Cap'n, go side-track yo'train!
> > (*Chicka-hanka, chicka-hanka, chicka-hanka!*)
> > Number Three in line,
> > A-comin' in on[1] time,
> Cap'n, go side-track yo' train!
> > (*Chicka-hanka, chicka-hanka, chicka-hanka!*)

[1]The O is pronounced long, like "ohn" or "ōn."

Chicka-hanka

Note. In male quartet, the tenors should sing the melody, the basses the refrain. Full male chorus should divide in the same way. The refrain should be sung softly (or almost spoken), with just enough tone to carry the consonants. It is merely an imitation of the sound of a slow-moving train – probably a heavy "freight"– being side-tracked to make room for "No. 3".

* "O" is pronounced long in Negro dialect: "ohn."

154

"HYAH, RATTLER!"

ANOTHER little example of how the song-loving black man sings about everything and anything, is offered in this bit of melody. In running across the field the Negro was bitten on the heel by a rattlesnake which then darted down a "holler lawg" (hollow log). The man calls his dog and it barks furiously—but we are not told whether or not the snake is driven from the "lawg" and killed; we only know that the incident, lingering in the mind of the man, was turned into a little song. It is probably a fact that the Negro *thinks* tunefully, so that in musing over any event it is natural for him to think aloud in song.

The slender little outline of melody in this snatch of tune contains the characteristic flat seventh; the grace-note at the end of the opening phrase marks an effort to express in notation the curious little high break in the voice (not altogether unlike the Swiss "yodel") in which the Negro often indulges and which really defies the recording pencil. When sung by quartet, or chorus, the solo voice sings the narrative, and the chorus comes in on the refrain "Hyah, Rattler, Hyah!"

"HYAH, RATTLER!"

A rattler went daown dat holler lawg,[1]
      Hyah![2] Rattler! Hyah!
   Ma dawg,[3]—Rattler!
   Ma dawg,—Rattler!
      Hyah! Rattler! Hyah!

As I was runnin' 'cross de fiel',
A rattlesnake bit me on[4] de heel,
      Hyah! Rattler! Hyah!
   Ow! Ow![5]—Hyah! Rattler!
   Ow! Ow!—Hyah! Rattler!
      Hyah! Rattler! Hyah!

[1]Hollow log.
[2]Here.
[3]Dog.
[4]The O is pronounced long, like "ohn" or "ōn."
[5]To imitate the barking of a dog.

"OLD RAGS, BOTTLES, RAGS!"

ONE morning I was awakened by the clanking of bells and the sound of a voice chanting a little snatch of a refrain. I looked out into a bright cloudless day and saw a battered old rubbish-cart drawn by a sleepy mule, coming slowly down the dusty road. A few crazy bells were strung above the cart and an old colored man sat on the box, lazily lashing the mule with a knotted piece of cord tied to the end of a stick. He was ragged and powdered with dust, and so was his animal, but both seemed utterly content to be ambling thus melodiously through the summer day. And as the old Negro threw his head back and warbled his refrain, with a little yodel-like break in his voice, it seemed to me as though he were singing to the sunshine—singing of the sheer, elemental joy of life, for the prosaic words of his song had melted away into pure euphony. He tuned his voice to chime with his jangling bells, for he sang in pitch with them, and he emphasized the irregular rhythms of his little chant with his ineffectual but decorative bit of cord, which he whirled in the air more as a matter of artistic enjoyment than for any effect that it might have upon the shuffling mule. He was only an old ragman, but his passing woke music on the roads and the memory of his happy voice and cheery bells still rings in my mind.

"Hyah, Rattler!"

A rat-tler went daown dat hol-ler lawg!____
Hyah, Rat - tler, hyah!
Ma dawg, Rat-tler, ma dawg, Rat-tler!
Hyah, Rat - tler, hyah!
As I was run - nin' 'cross de fiel',____
A rat-tle-snake bit me on de heel.____
Hyah, Rat - tler, hyah!
Ow! Ow! Hyah, Rat - tler, Ow! Ow! Hyah, Rat - tler!
Hyah, Rat - tler, hyah!

"Old Rags, Bottles, Rags!"

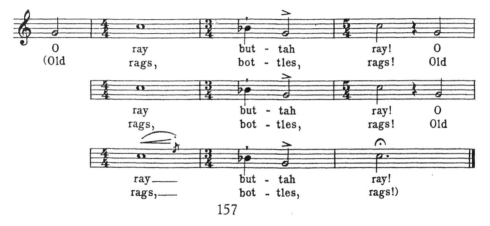

O ray but - tah ray! O
(Old rags, bot - tles, rags! Old

ray but - tah ray! O
rags, bot - tles, rags! Old

ray____ but - tah ray!
rags,____ bot - tles, rags!)

'LIZA-JANE

DANCE-GAME SONG

("Stealin' Partners")

THIS is a dance-game, not unlike the "Oats-peas-beans" of childhood. A number of couples, men and women, dance in a circle, in the centre of which an extra man, who has no partner, dances alone. The performance of this solo dancer is adorned with elaborate, loose-jointed pattering steps, while stamps, turns and flings add emphasis to the throbbing accentuation of the music. The object of the game is for the lone man in the middle of the ring to steal a partner from one of the men in the dancing circle. Then the robbed man must take the centre, and it now becomes his turn to find a mate. So the game goes on, with a constant shifting of partners, while each solo dancer vies with his predecessors in a marvellous abandonment of dance-improvisation.

Any number of verses may be made up to suit the occasion. The song is old, but some of the lines here given are very apparently modern, for we may well believe that it is only in recent years that the "house in Baltimo'" has acquired a "Brussels carpet on de flo'" and a "silver door-plate on de do'". If the Negroes continue to dance this quaint old game, no doubt the historic house will be brought still further "up-to-date."

This is one of those Negro songs whose rhythmic accompaniment of stamping, shuffling feet and hand-clapping seems an intrinsic part of its musical character. Yet as the dance-step is not fixed, but extemporaneous, I have been able only to indicate a sort of synopsis, as it were, of the different beats, approximating the rhythms of the dancing feet. It would seem, too, as though no record of the song could be complete without some indication of the bursts of laughter and the shouts and calls whose jolly noise colors the simple little tune; for the game of "Stealin' Partners" always forms the groundwork for hilarious fun. The jokes played, the verses improvised, the fantasy and extravaganza of loosened high spirits—all this, which escapes notation and defies description, is at the same time part of the song. The elasticity of the Negro voice finds full play in embellishing with part-singing the shouted chorus. The tenor soars up a tenth above the voice of the "lead" with the same full-throated joy in sound that prompts the bass to dip a tenth below the baritone. Such a volume of tone as pours from those open, laughing mouths, lit by the flash of white teeth!

The onlooker, gazing and listening, is swept by the gale of good-nature that blows across the dance, and is brought to realize how inextinguishable is the cheerfulness and summer-day humor of the black man. Scarcely a race in history—with the exception of the Jews—has suffered greater oppression and wrong; yet in spite of bondage and sorrow, no people in the world seem to have a greater faculty for utter childlike enjoyment than the Negroes at play.

'LIZA-JANE

("Stealin' Partners")

Come ma love an' go wid me,
      L'il' 'Liza-Jane,
Come ma love an' go wid me,
      L'il' 'Liza-Jane.

    O Eliza,[1]
      L'il' 'Liza-Jane,
    O Eliza,
      L'il' 'Liza-Jane.

I got a house in Baltimo',
      L'il' 'Liza-Jane,
Street-car runs right by ma do',
      L'il' 'Liza-Jane.

    O Eliza,
      L'il' 'Liza-Jane,
    O Eliza,
      L'il' 'Liza-Jane.

I got a house in Baltimo',
      L'il' 'Liza-Jane,
Brussels carpet on[2] de flo',
      L'il' 'Liza-Jane.

    O Eliza,
      L'il' 'Liza-Jane,
    O Eliza,
      L'il' 'Liza-Jane.

I got a house in Baltimo',
      L'il' 'Liza-Jane,
Silver door-plate on de do',
      L'il' 'Liza-Jane.

    O Eliza,
      L'il' 'Liza-Jane,
    O Eliza,
      L'il' 'Liza-Jane.

[1]Sometimes "O Miss 'Liza" is sung instead of "O Eliza."
[2]The O is pronounced long—"ohn" or "ōn"—in Negro dialect.

'Liza-Jane

Dance-game Song

("Stealin' Partners")

Note. This song may be sung by solo and quartet; or by solo, quartet and chorus, the quartet singing the refrain "Li'l' 'Liza Jane", interspersed between the solo bars, and the full chorus coming in with "O, Eliza!" For concert performance it would be well to have the dance-rhythms indicated by a bone-player, and if he be a Negro, he can improvise his own rhythms with doubtless far more dynamic effect than any recorder could transcribe.

✱ The voice of the "Lead" carries the melody and is written in the piano-part in large type.

Chorus*

* When a number of people are dancing, all join in the chorus, and sometimes "O Eliza" is shouted at the top of their lungs. As this is a dance-song, dynamics are all broad, and consist chiefly in vociferous rhythmic accentuation. "O, *Miss* Liza" is sometimes sung instead of "O *E*-liza," and the Tenors may be made interchangeable with the different verses.

161

* For concert performance it will perhaps be found effective to sing the chorus through this time *pp*.

163

A little louder and bolder

Li'l 'Li - za Jane,

I got a house in Bal-ti-mo', Li'l 'Li - za Jane,

Li'l 'Li - za Jane,

Li'l 'Li - za Jane,

Li'l 'Li - za Jane.

Brus-sels car-pit on de flo', Li'l 'Li - za Jane.

Li'l 'Li - za Jane.

Li'l 'Li - za Jane.

* *O* in Negro dialect pronounced· long:"ohn".

164

At Hampton the following variant is sometimes used:

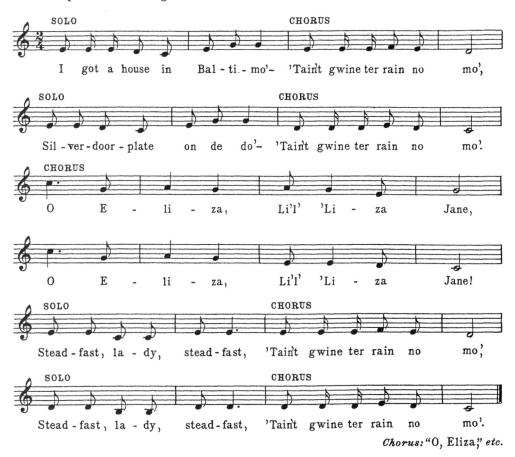

SOLO I got a house in Bal-ti-mo'- CHORUS 'Taint gwine ter rain no mo',

SOLO Sil-ver-door-plate on de do'- CHORUS 'Taint gwine ter rain no mo'.

CHORUS O E-li-za, Li'l' 'Li-za Jane,

O E-li-za, Li'l' 'Li-za Jane!

SOLO Stead-fast, la-dy, stead-fast, CHORUS 'Taint gwine ter rain no mo',

SOLO Stead-fast, la-dy, stead-fast, CHORUS 'Taint gwine ter rain no mo'.

Chorus: "O, Eliza," *etc.*

Charles N. Wheeler, writing in the Chicago Tribune, says that he heard the following words sung to the tune of "'Liza Jane" by the Negro soldiers in France, though the logical sequence of the lines seems to be reversed.

> "I'se got a gal an' you got none –
>   Li'l' 'Liza Jane,
> House an' lot in Baltimo'–
>   Li'l' 'Liza Jane,
> Lots o' chillnn round mah do'–
>   Li'l' 'Liza Jane.
> Th' bumblebee out for sip –
>   Li'l' 'Liza Jane,
> Takes th' sweetnin' from yo' lips –
>   Li'l' 'Liza Jane.
> Come, mah love, an' live with me –
>   Li'l' 'Liza Jane,
> An' I'll take good care of thee –
>   Li'l' 'Liza Jane."